ADULT COLORING BOOKS

Mandalas & Butterflies

Copyright © 2018

All rights reserved. No part of this book may be reproduced in any form whatsoever, stored in a retrieval system, now known or to be invented, or transmitted in any form or by any means, electronic, mechanical, photocopying, recording, scanning, or otherwise, without the prior written permission of the author or publisher.

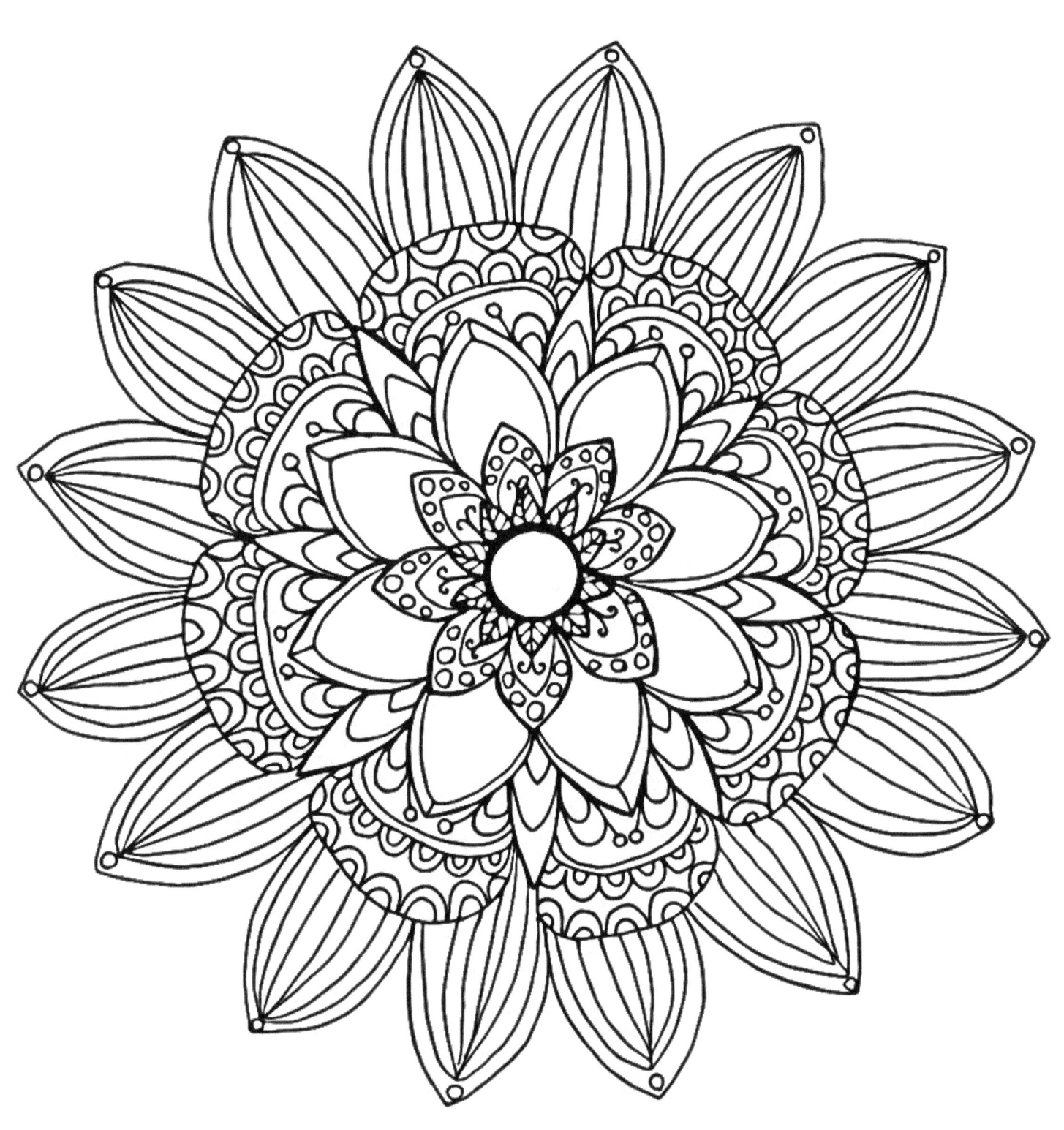

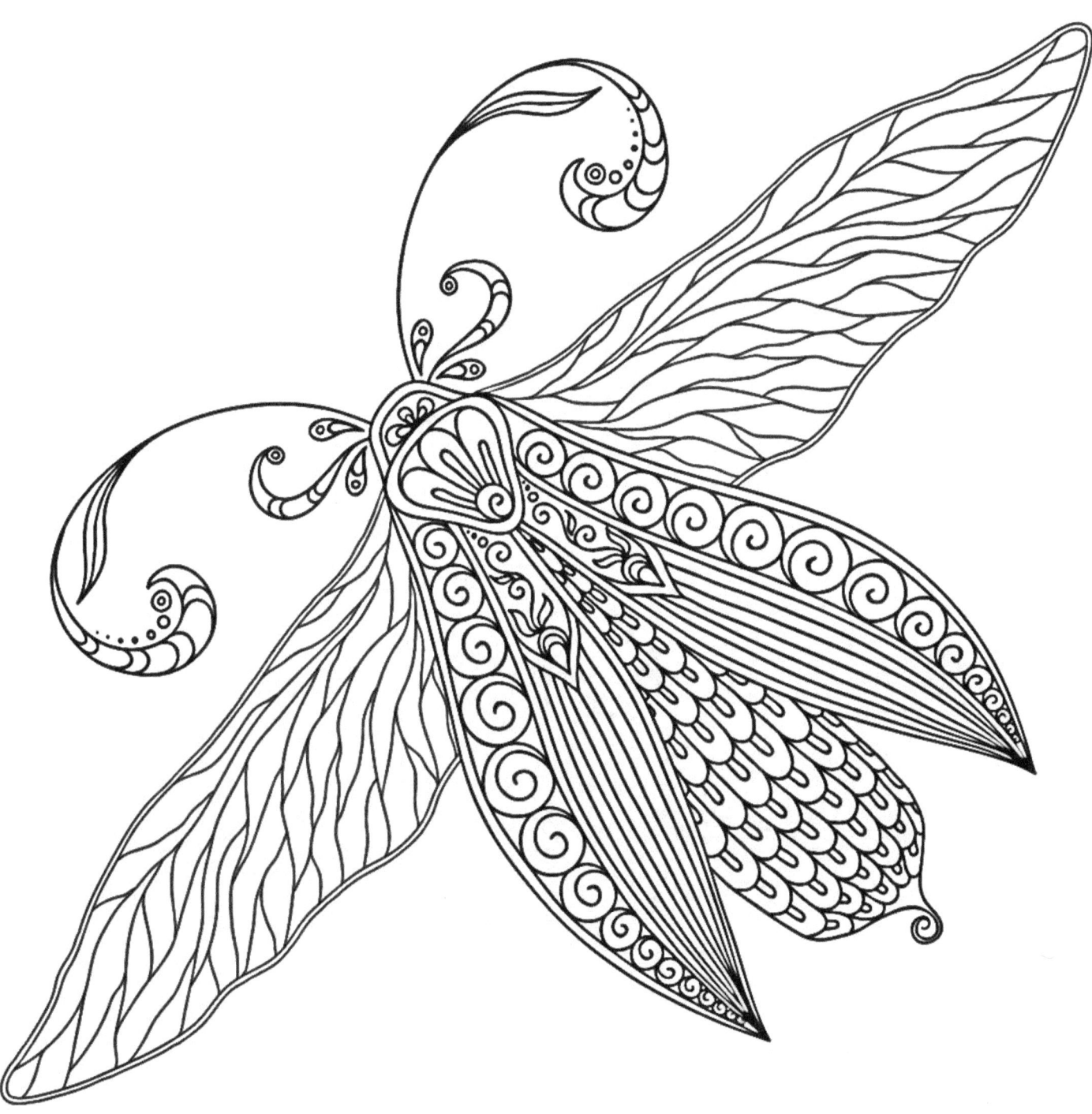

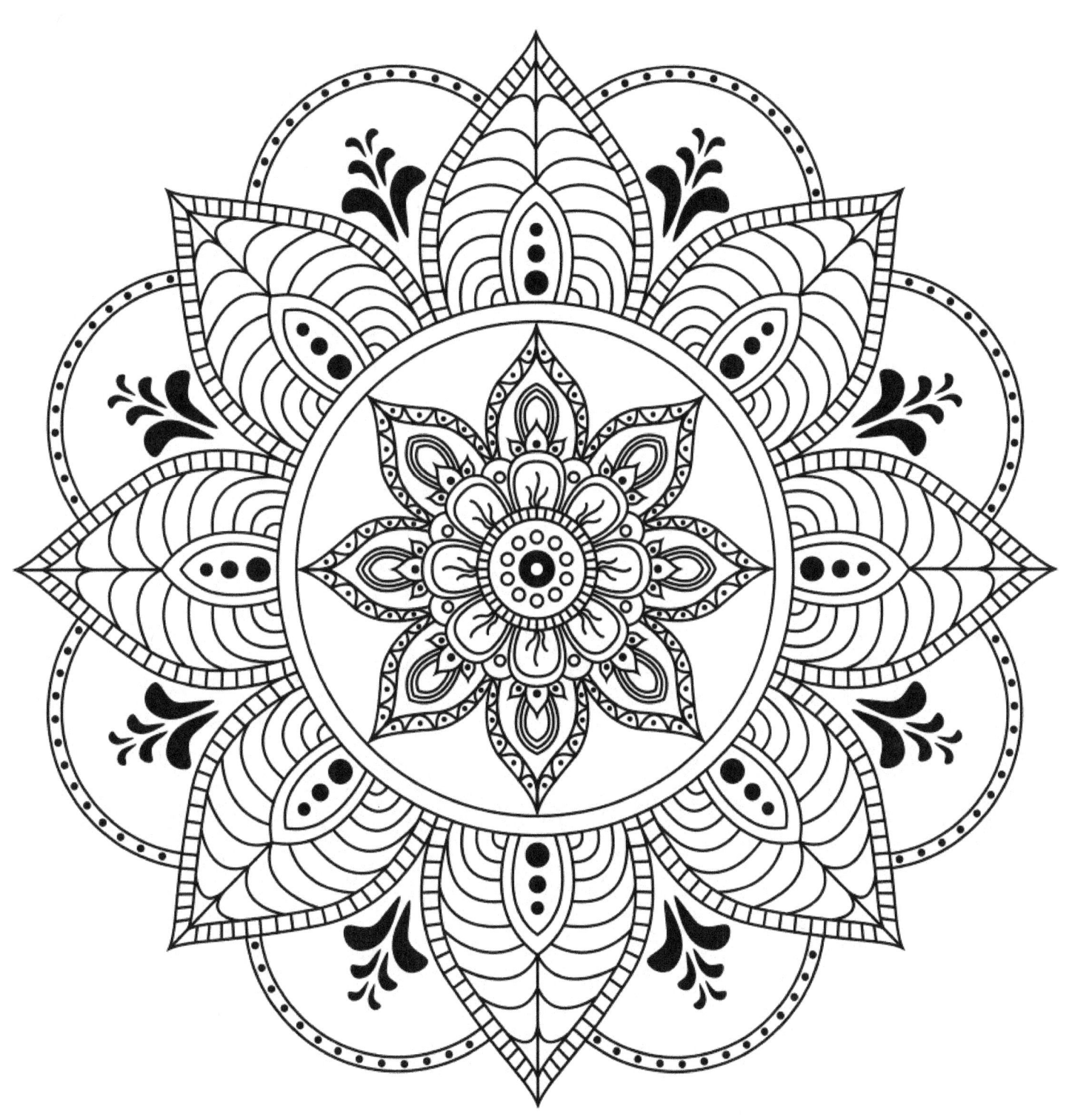

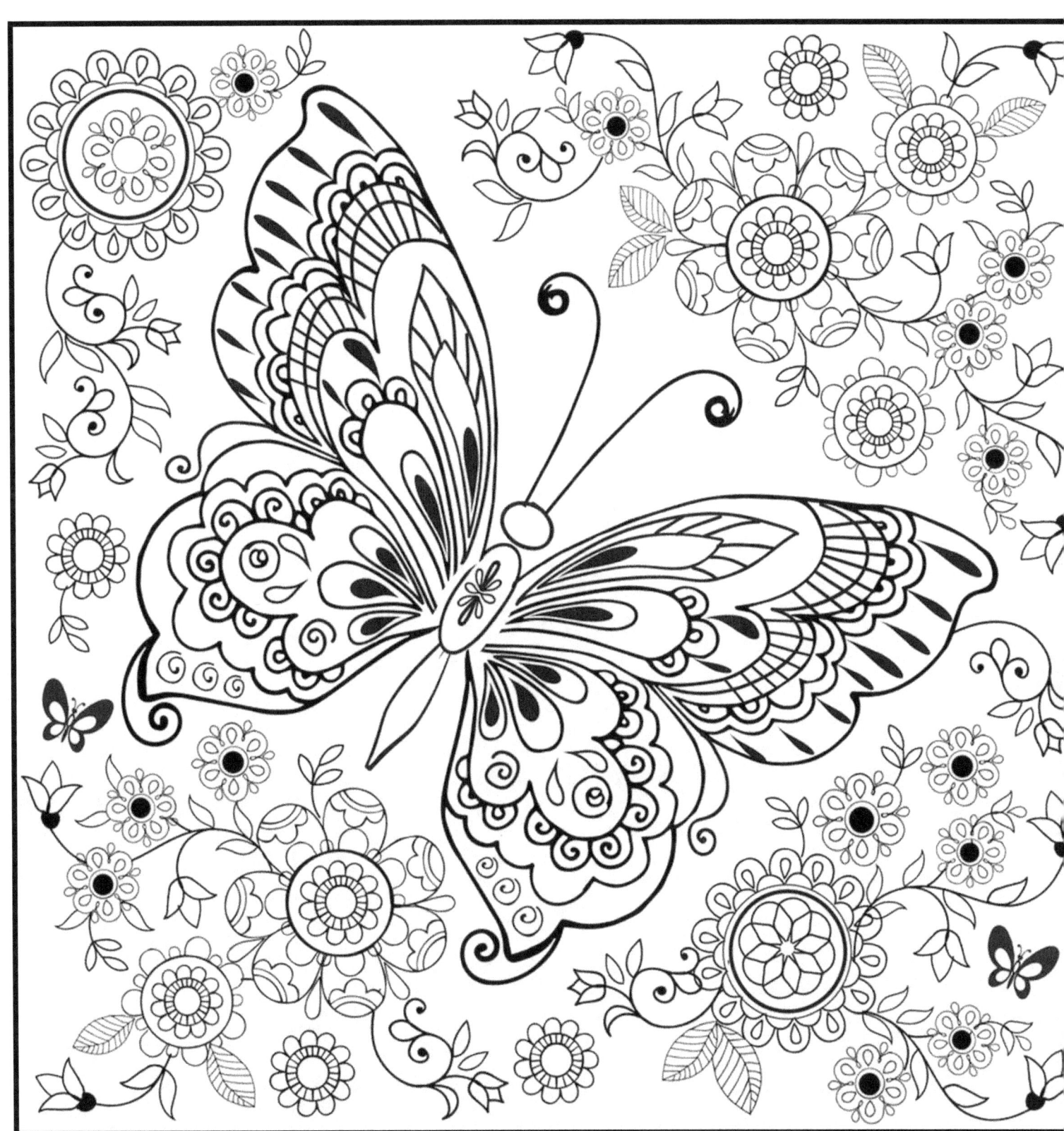

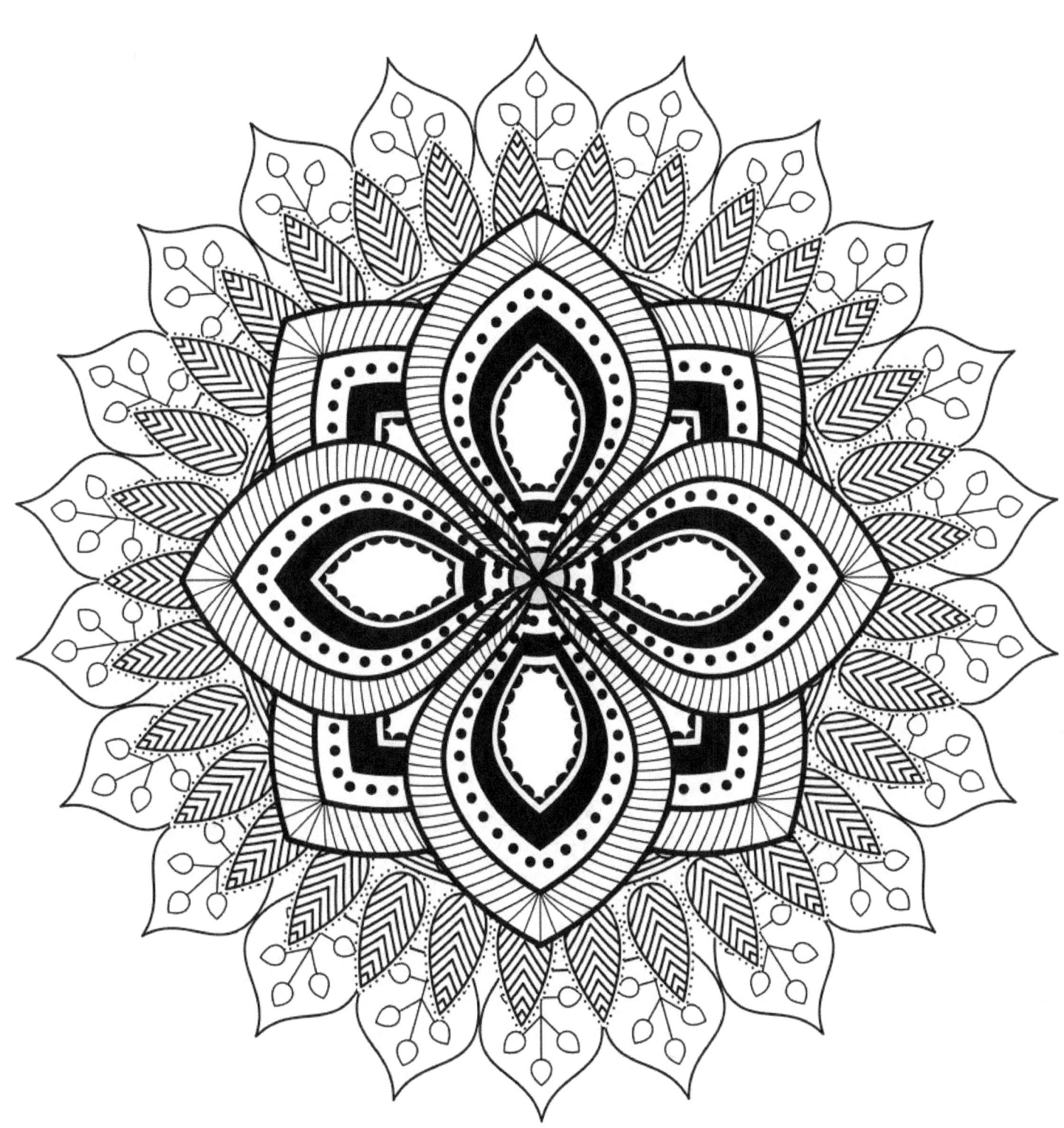

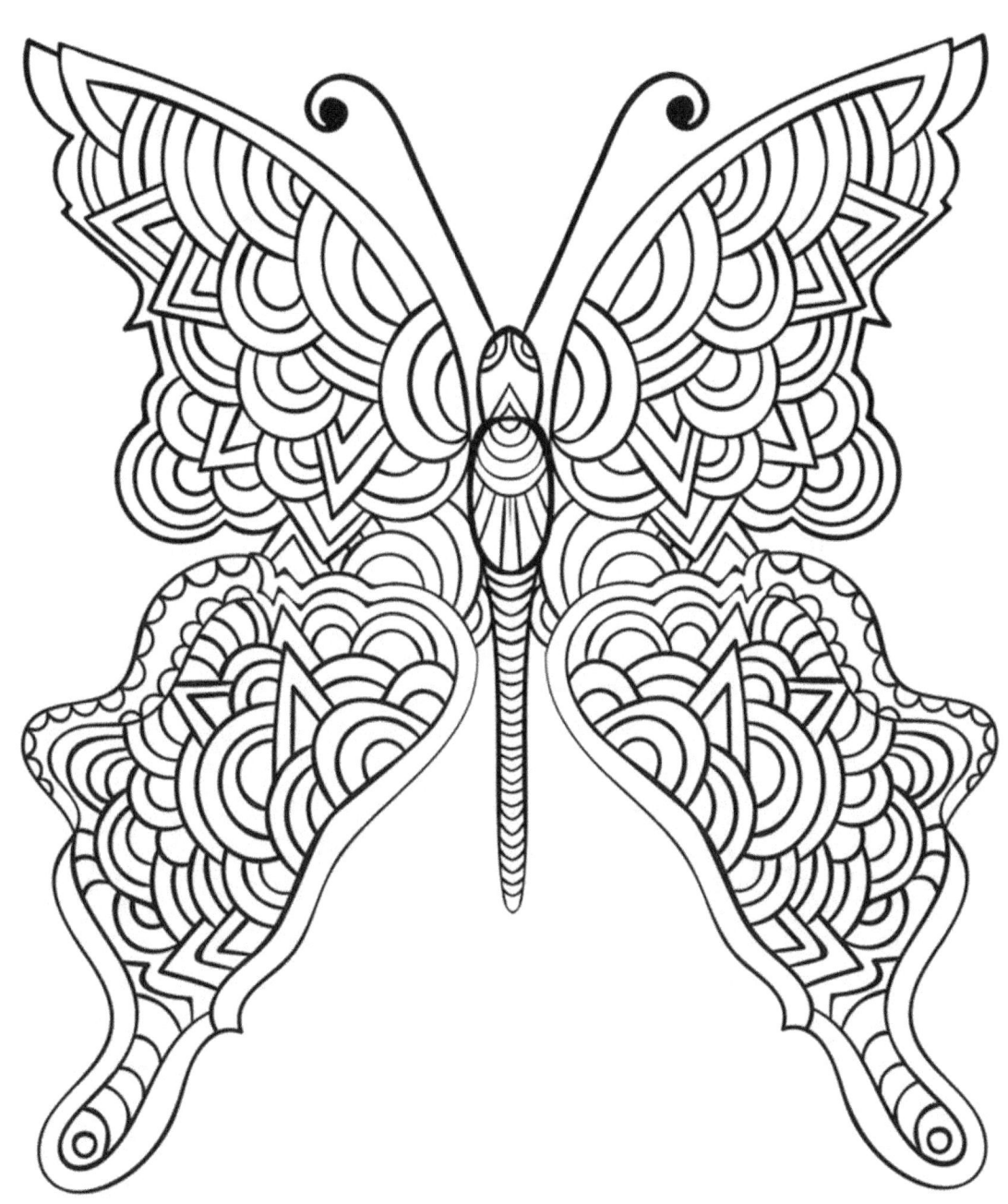

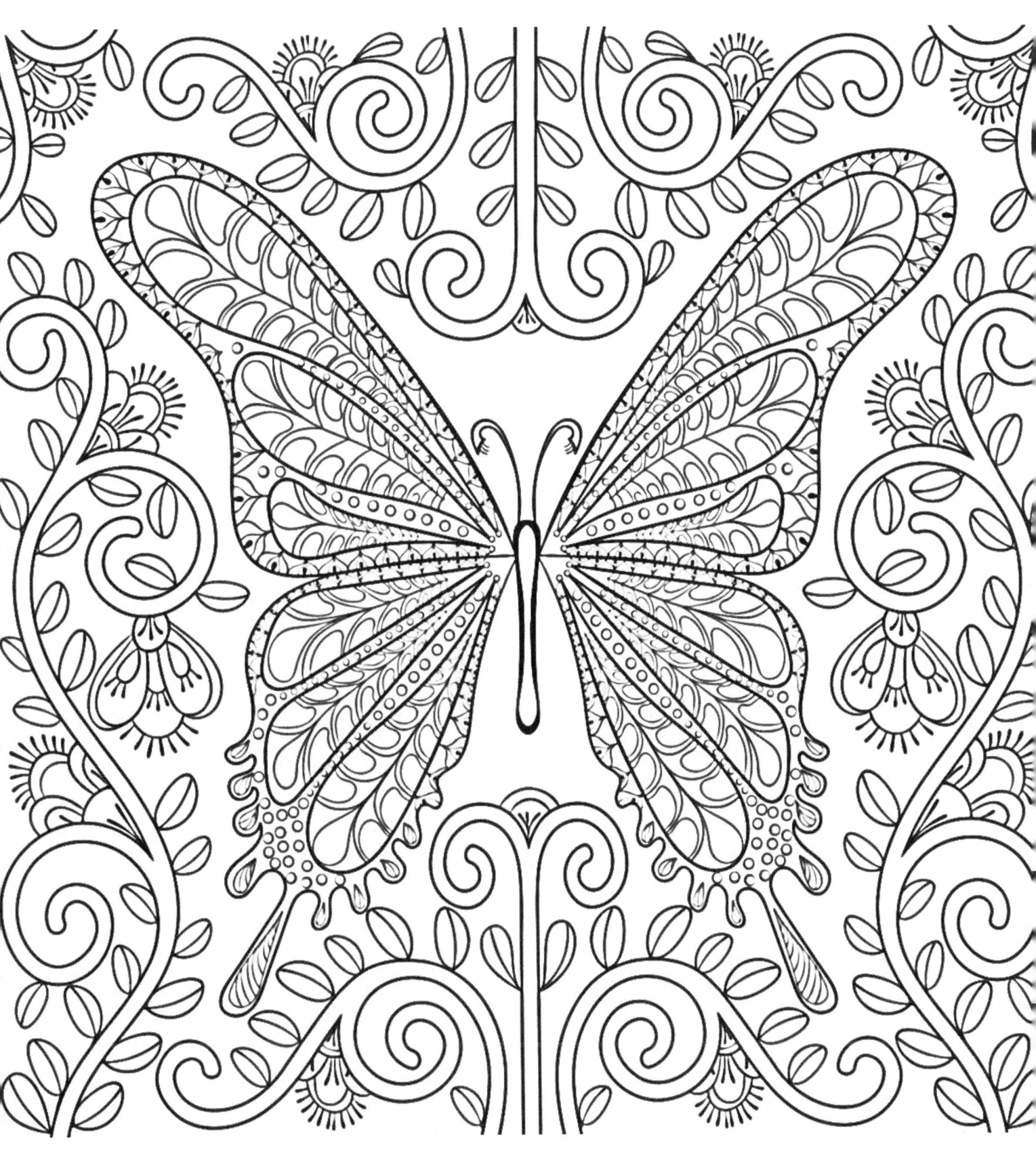

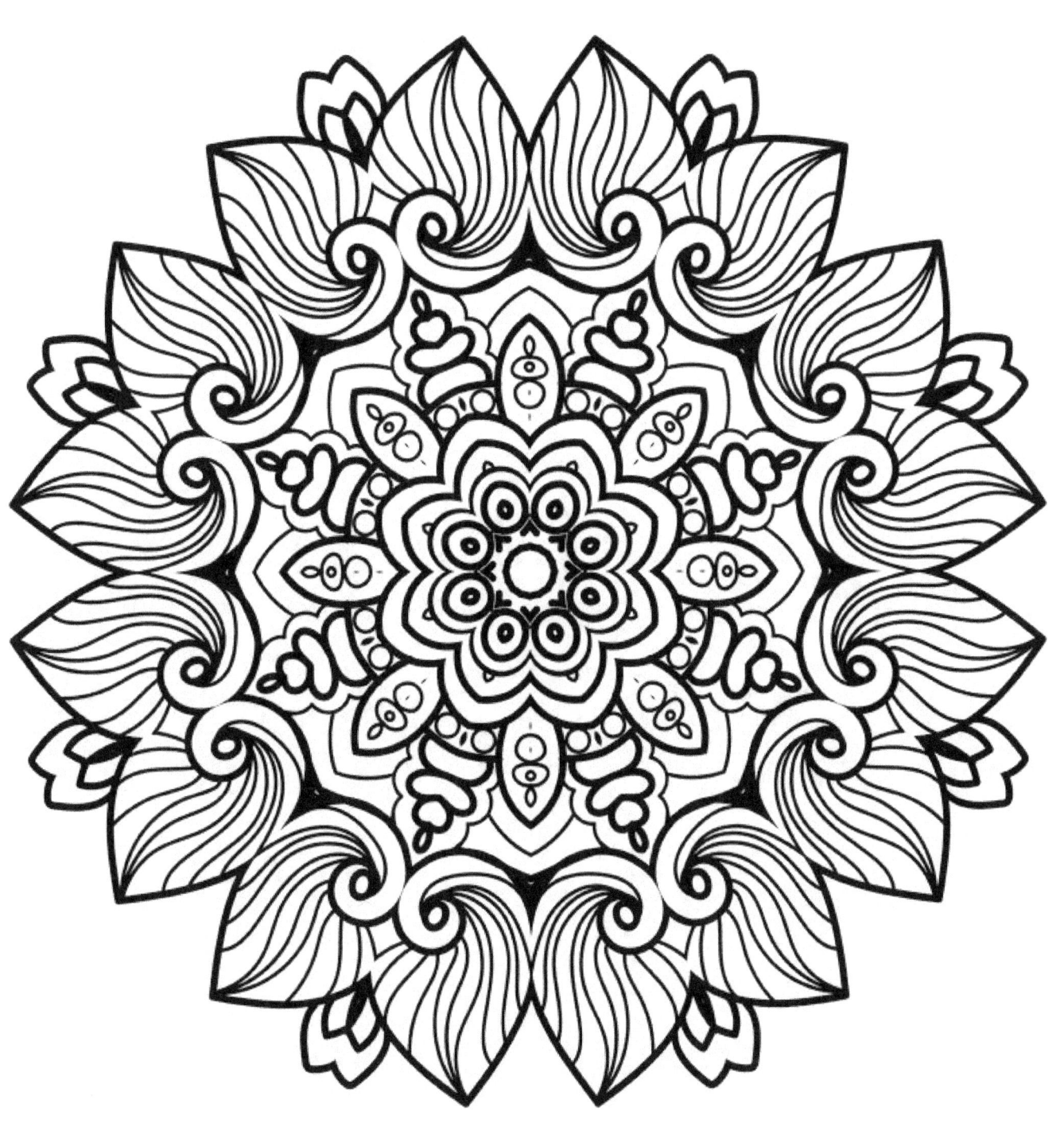

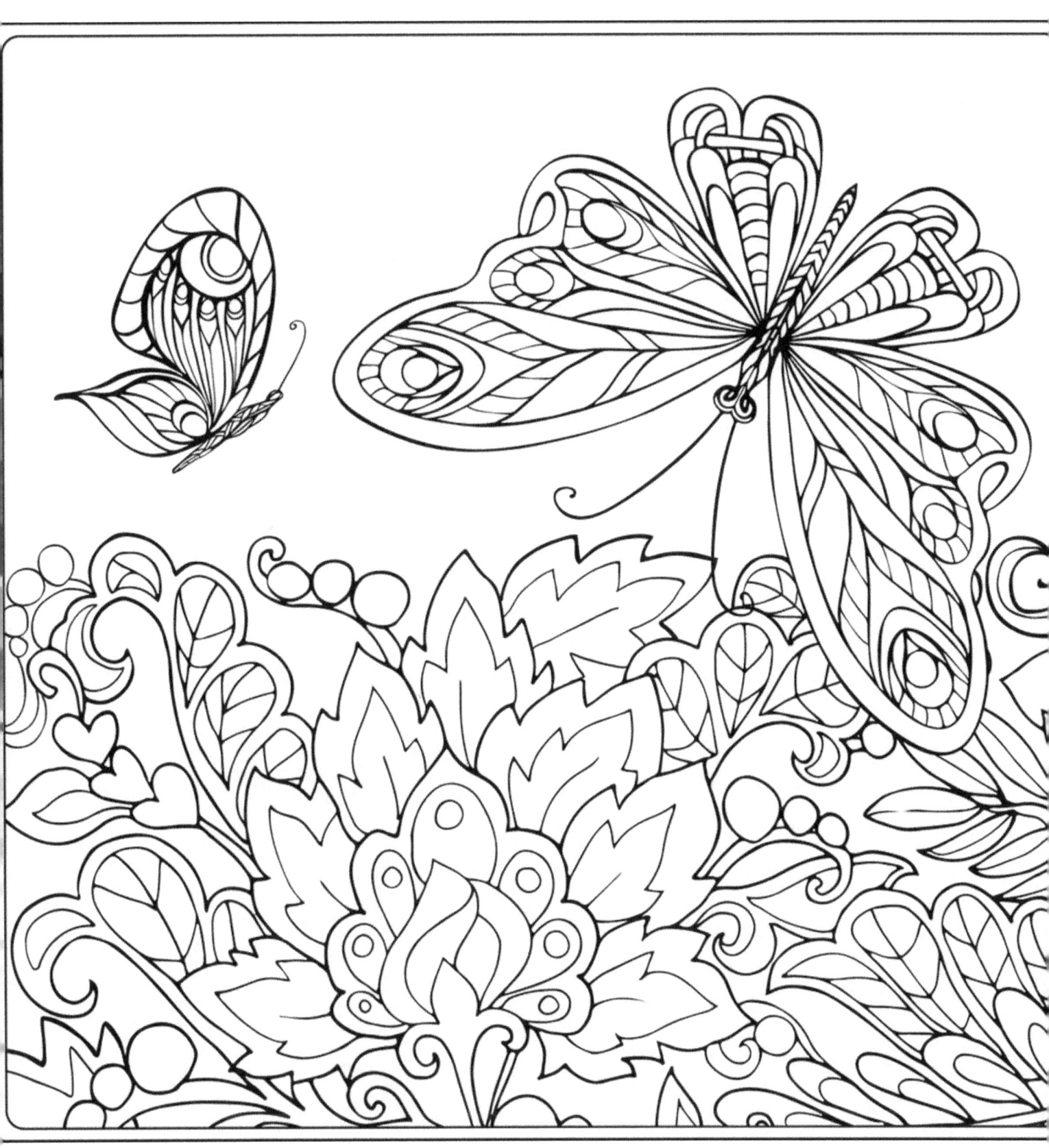

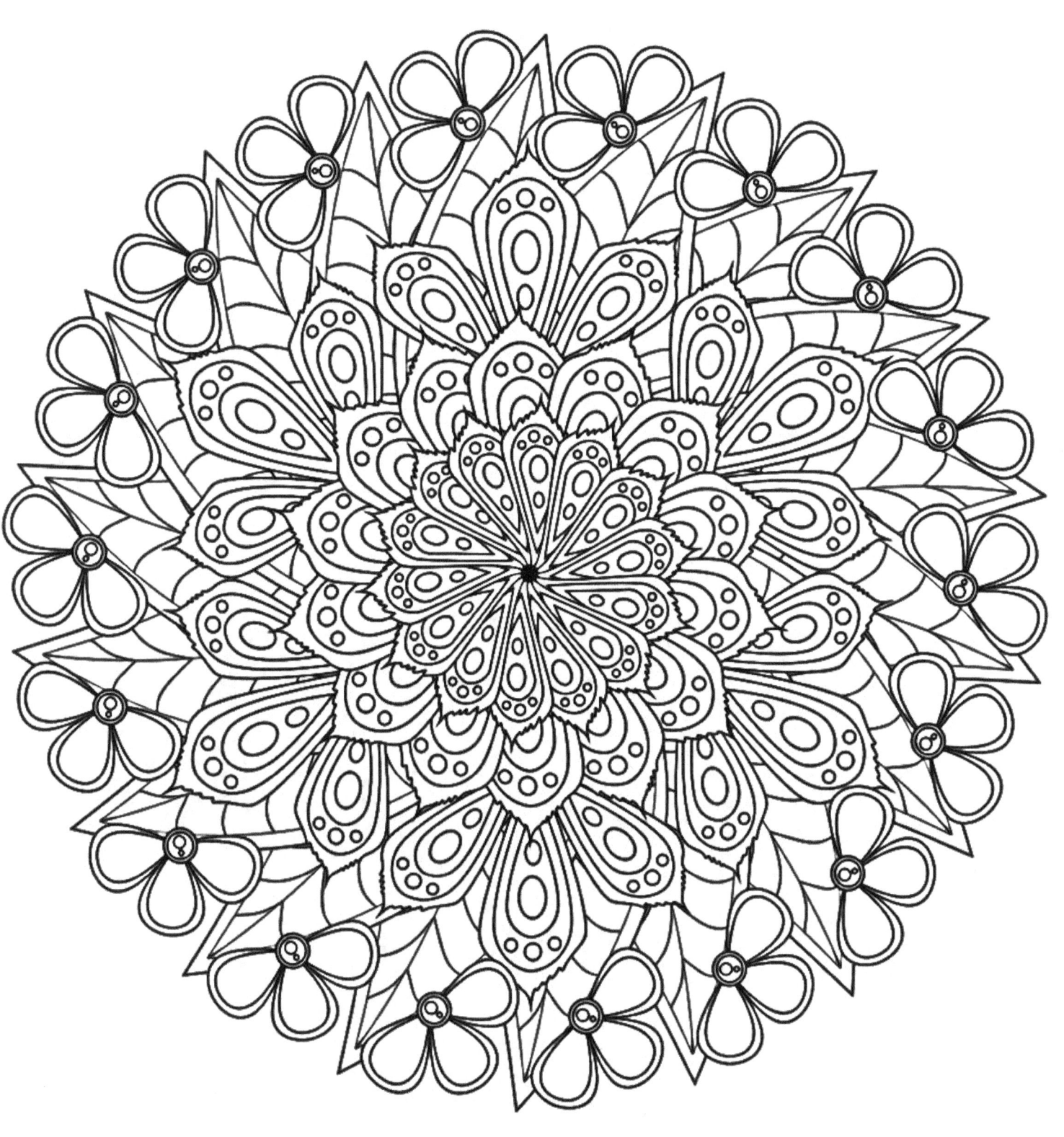

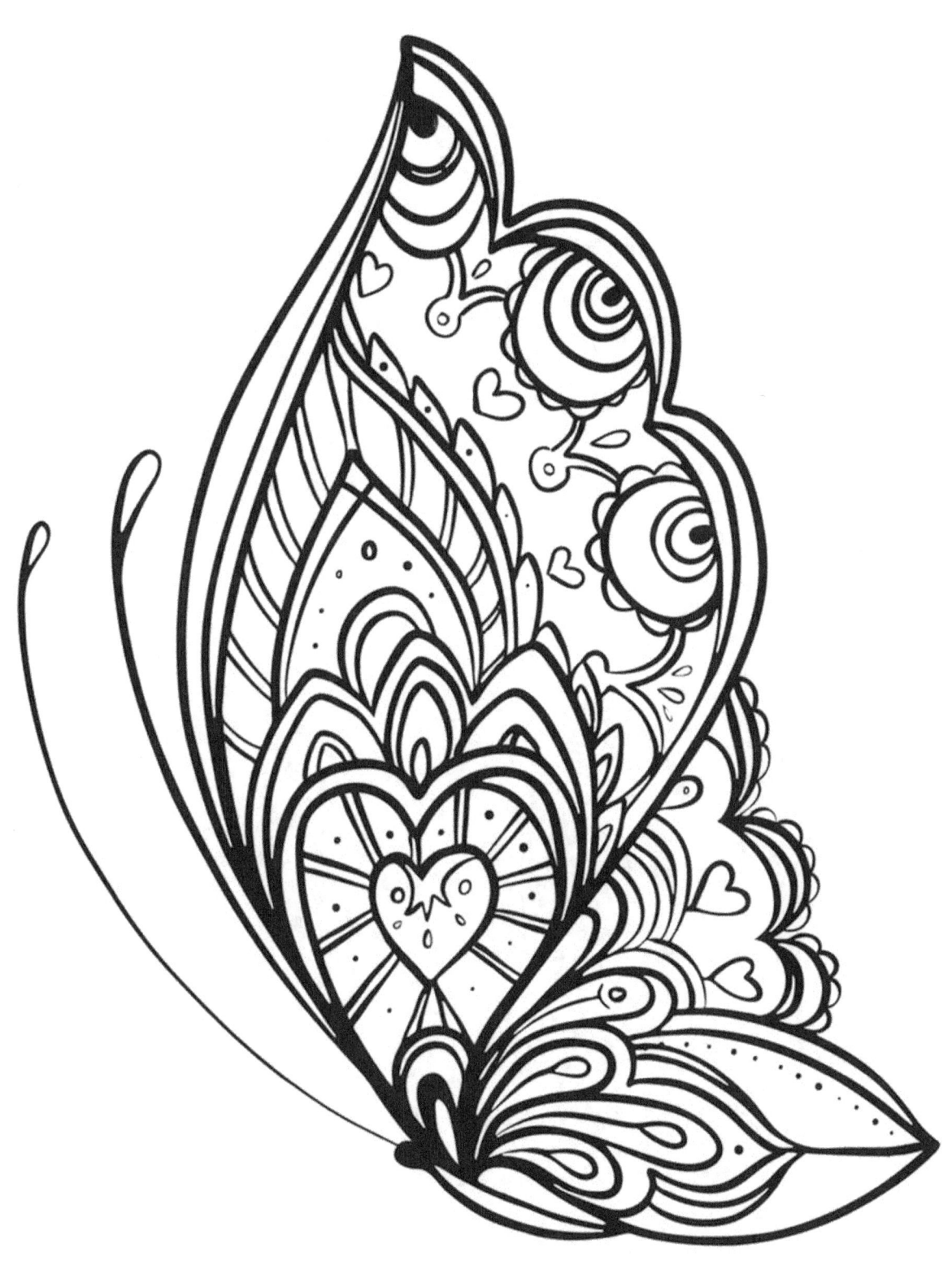

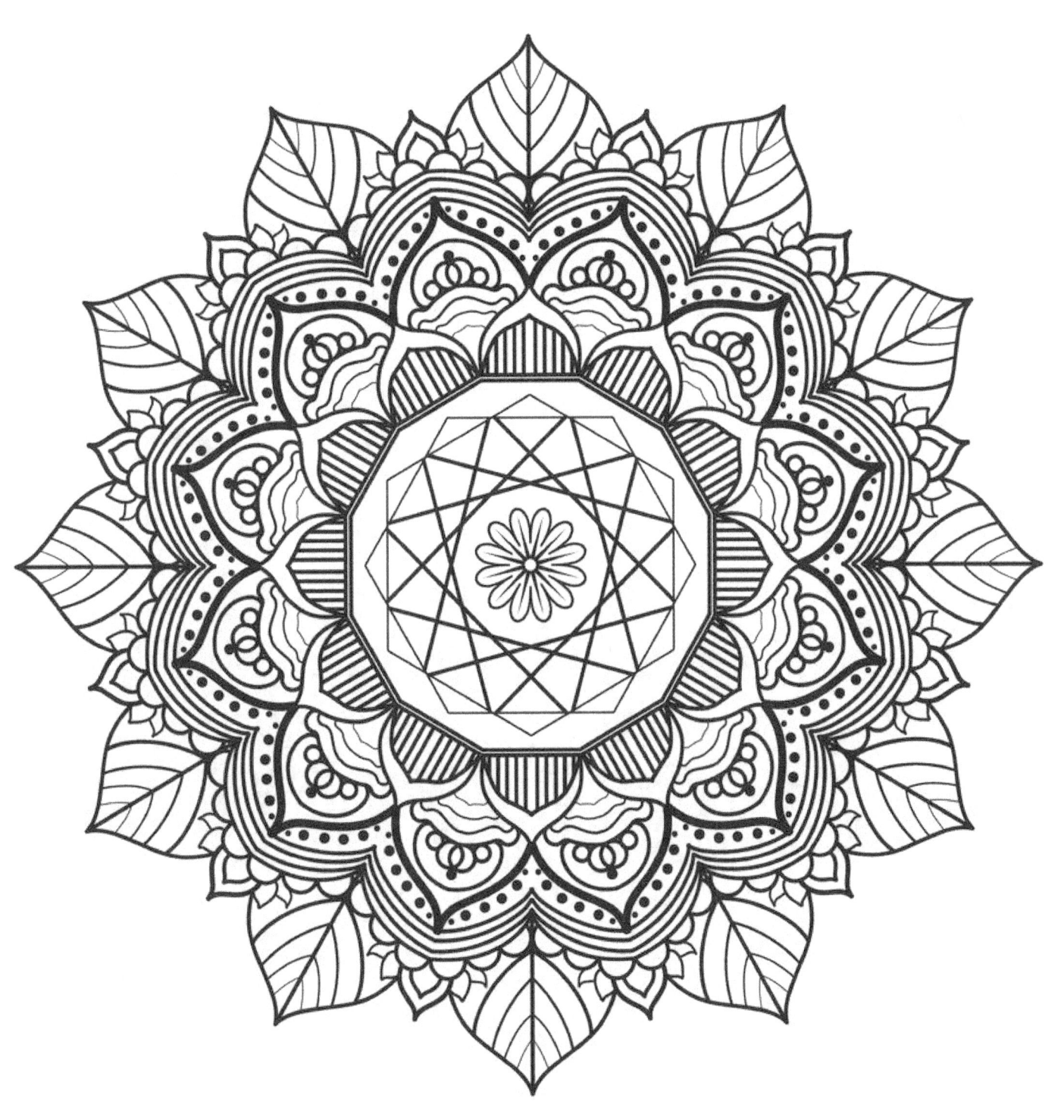

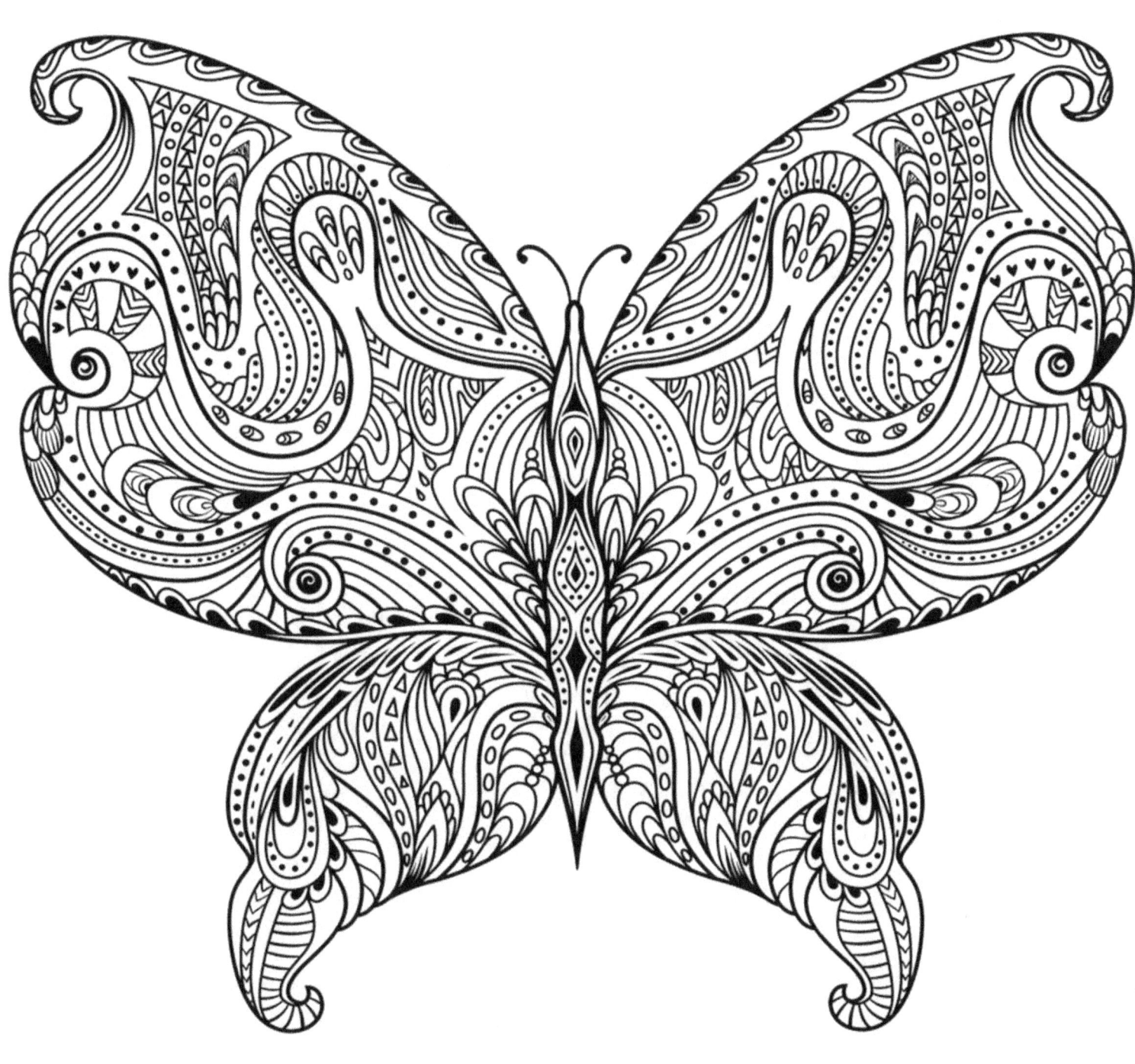

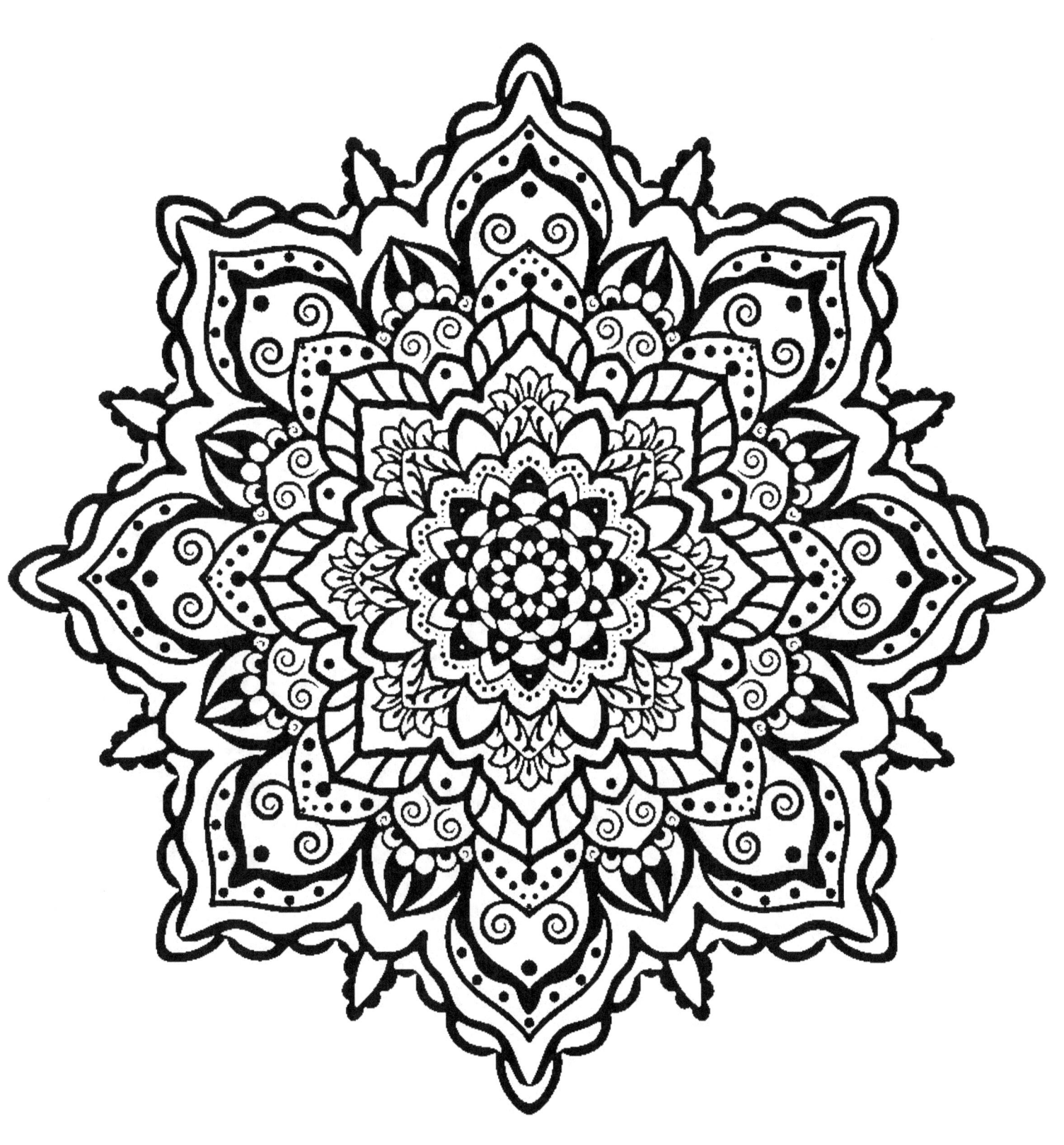

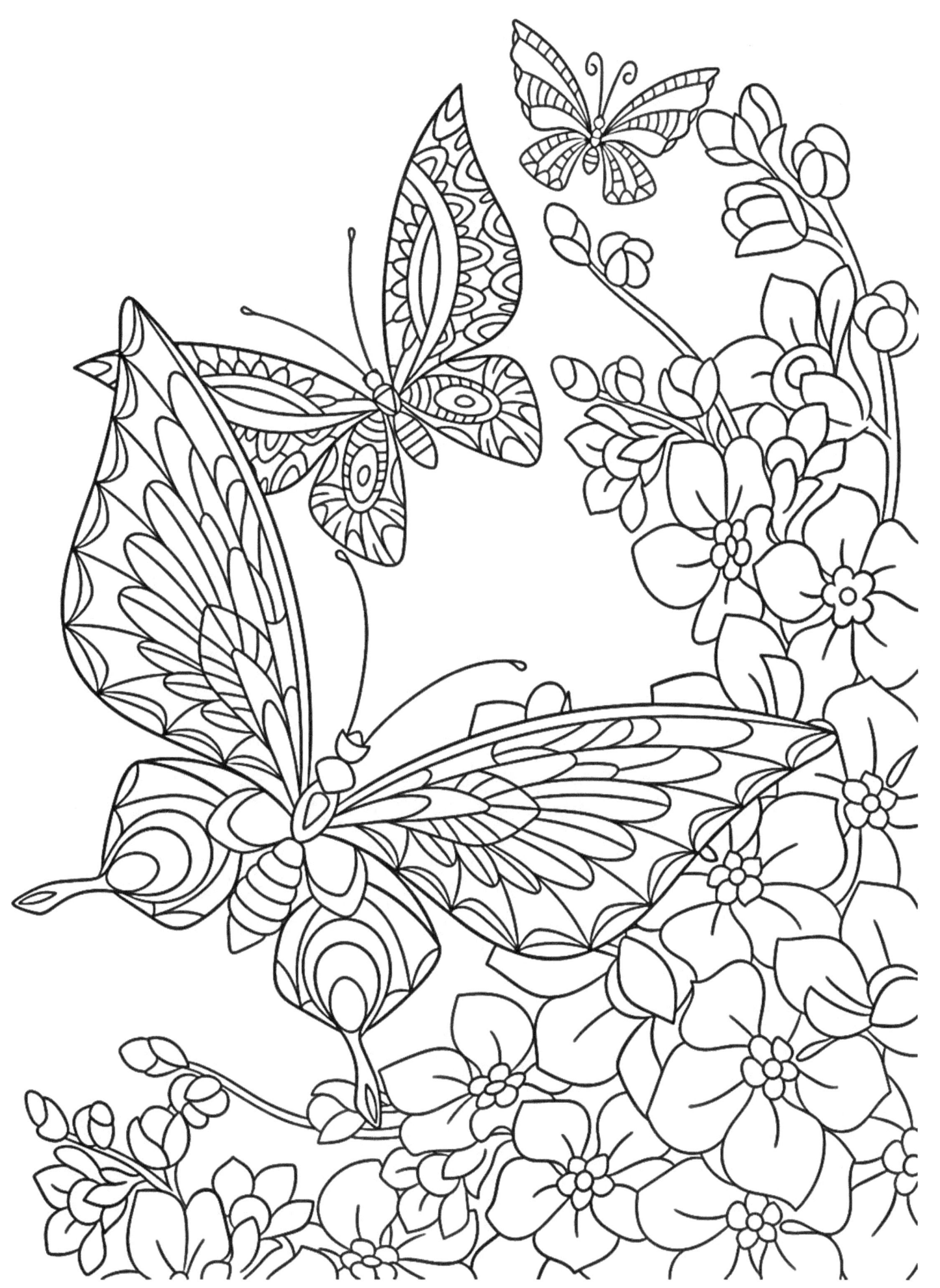

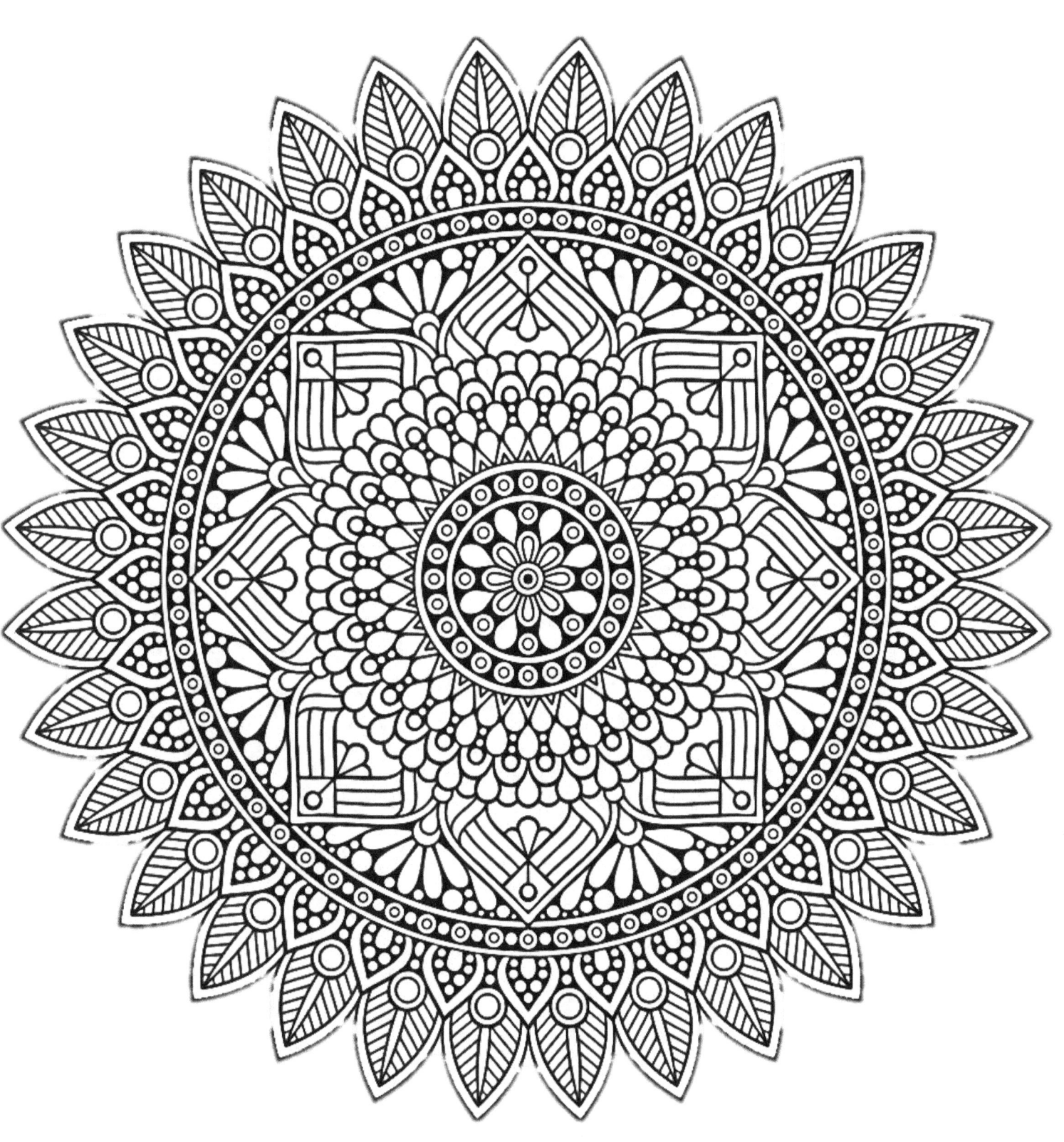

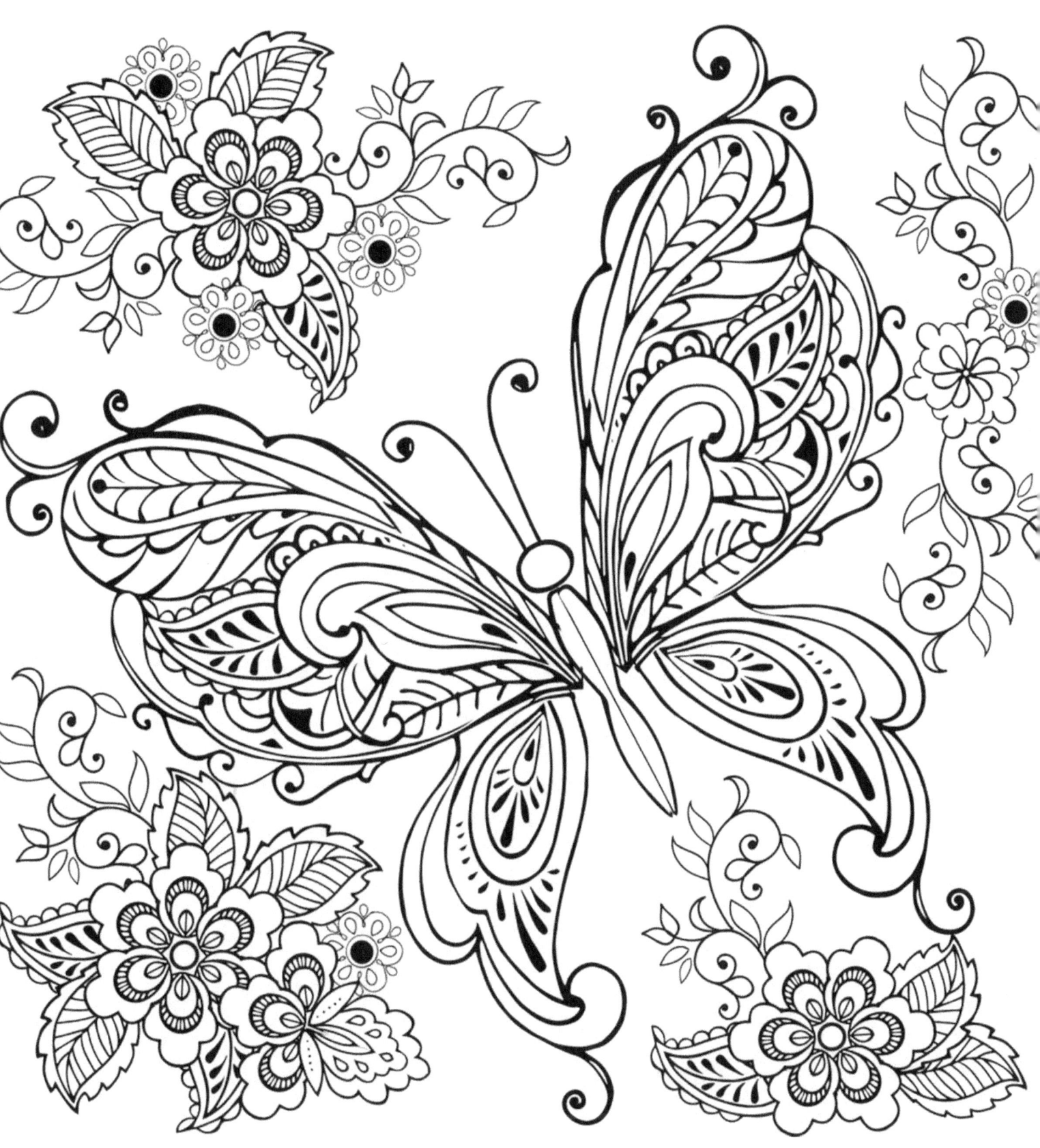

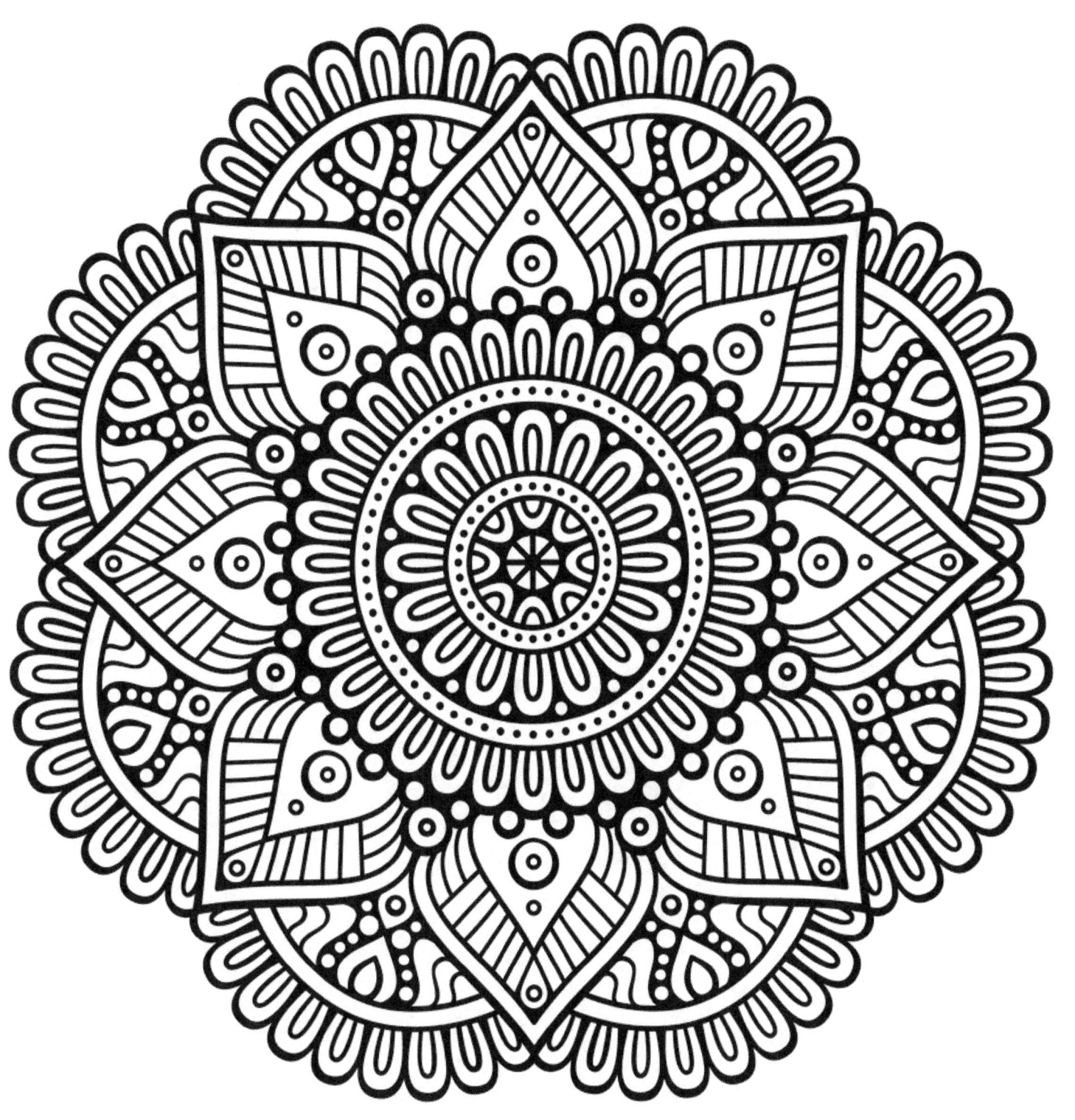

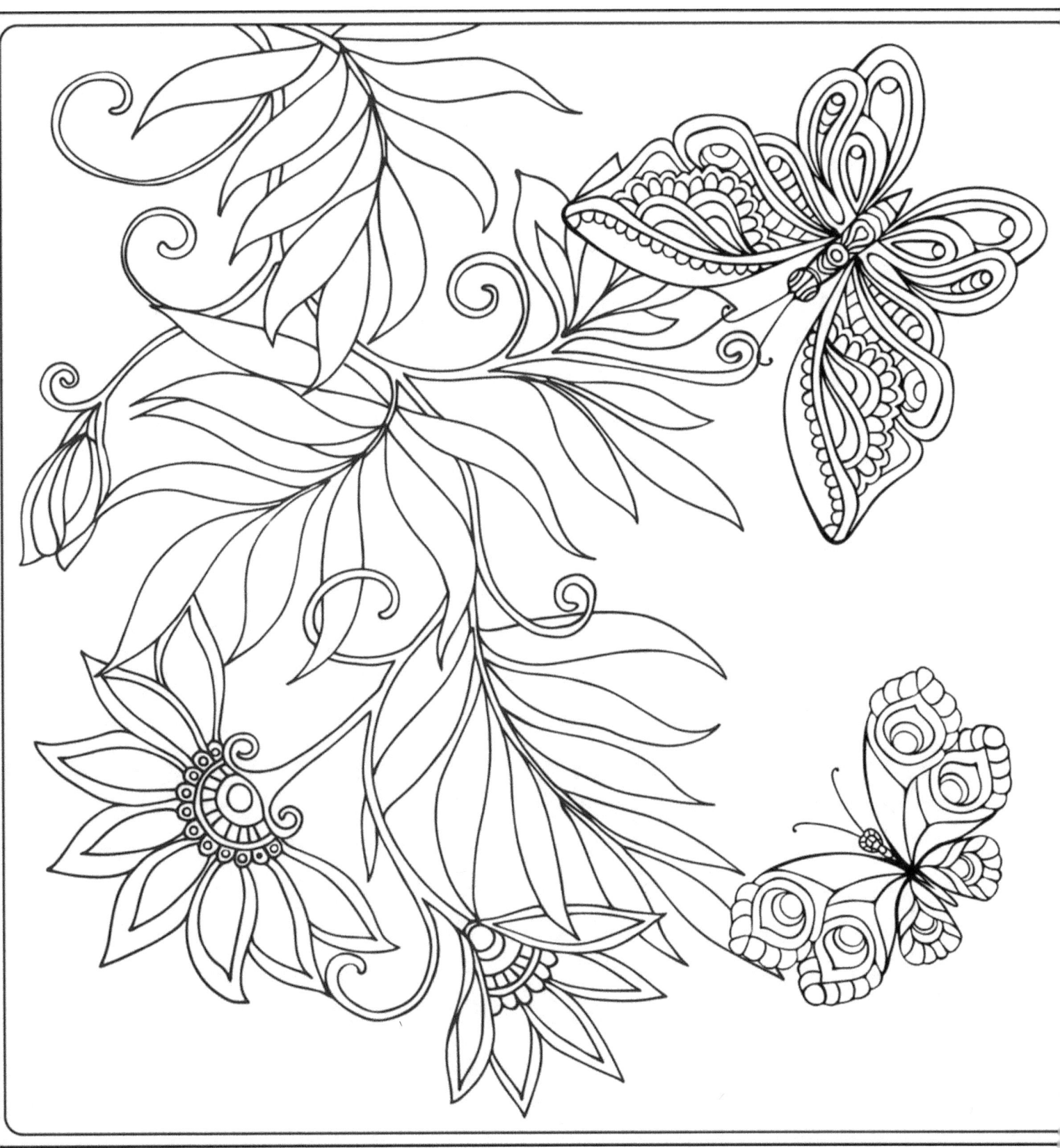

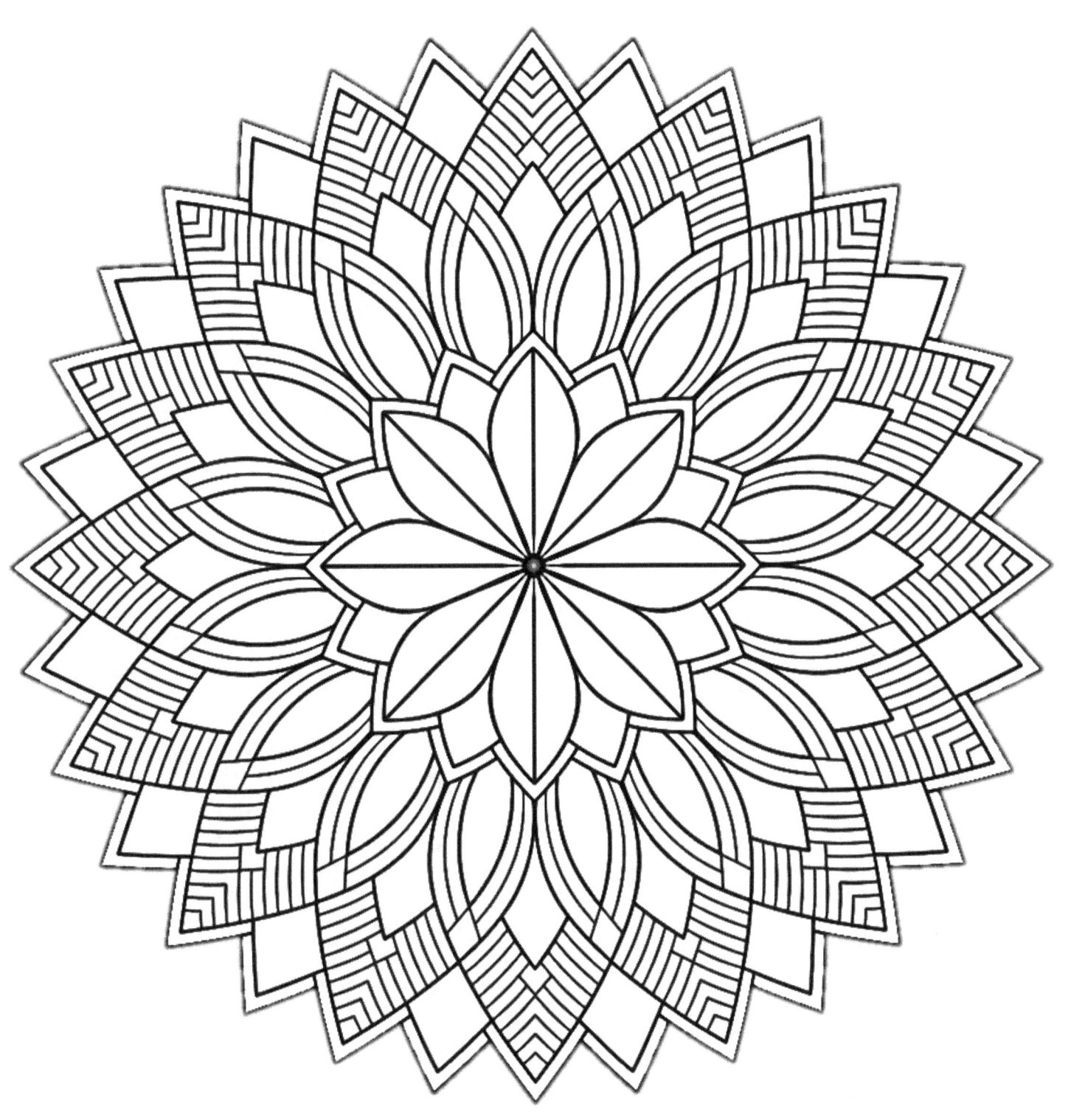

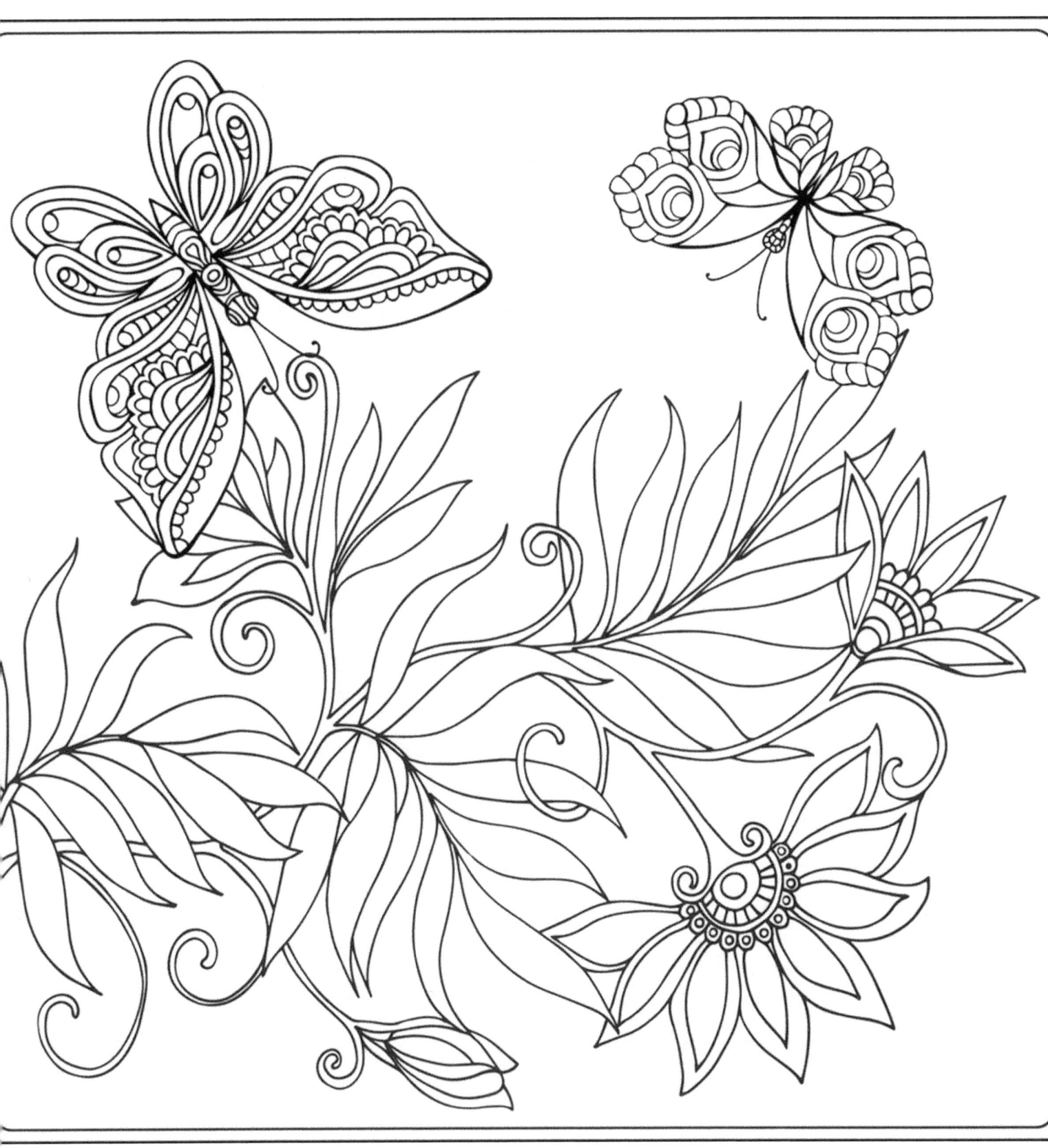

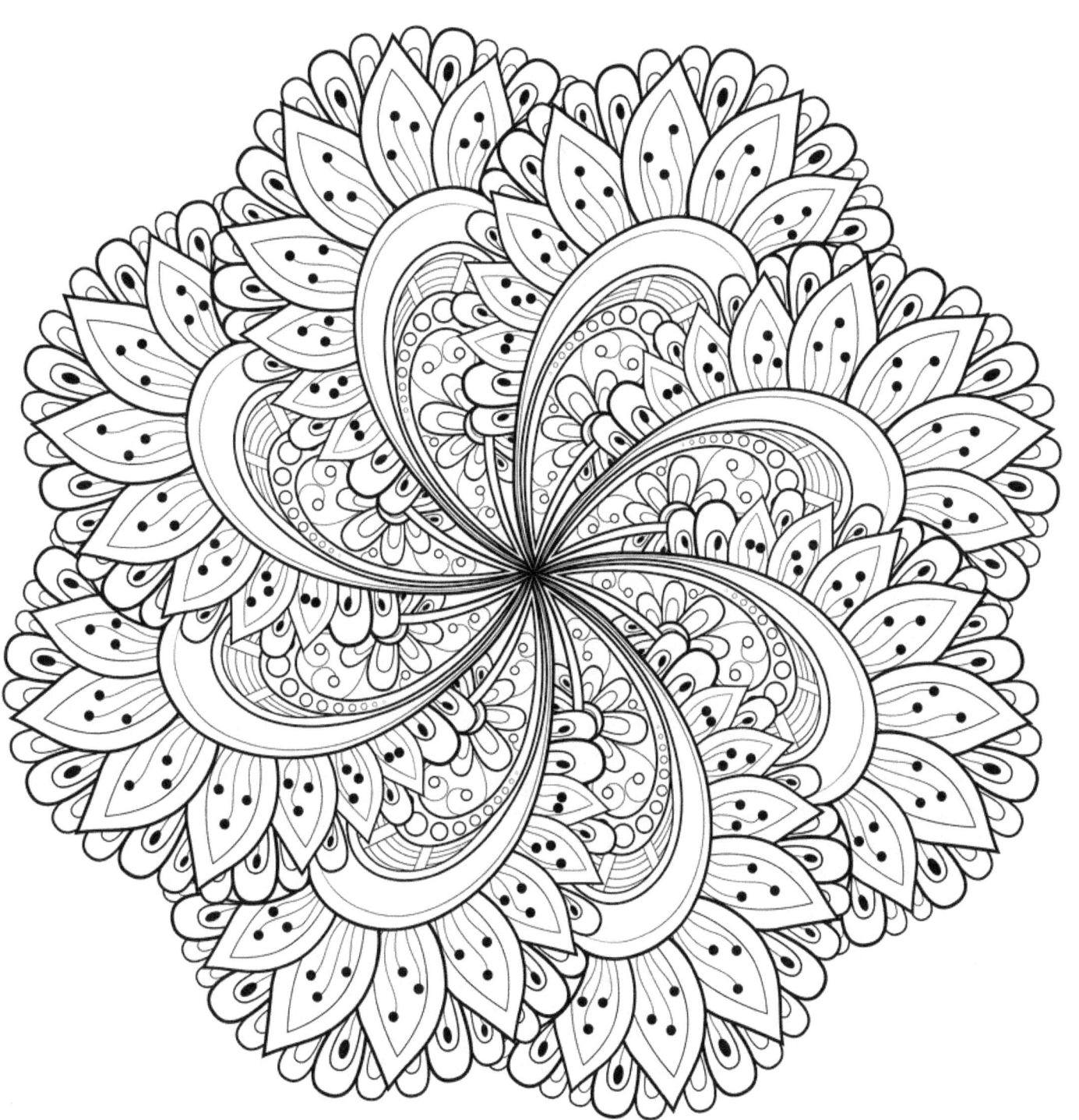

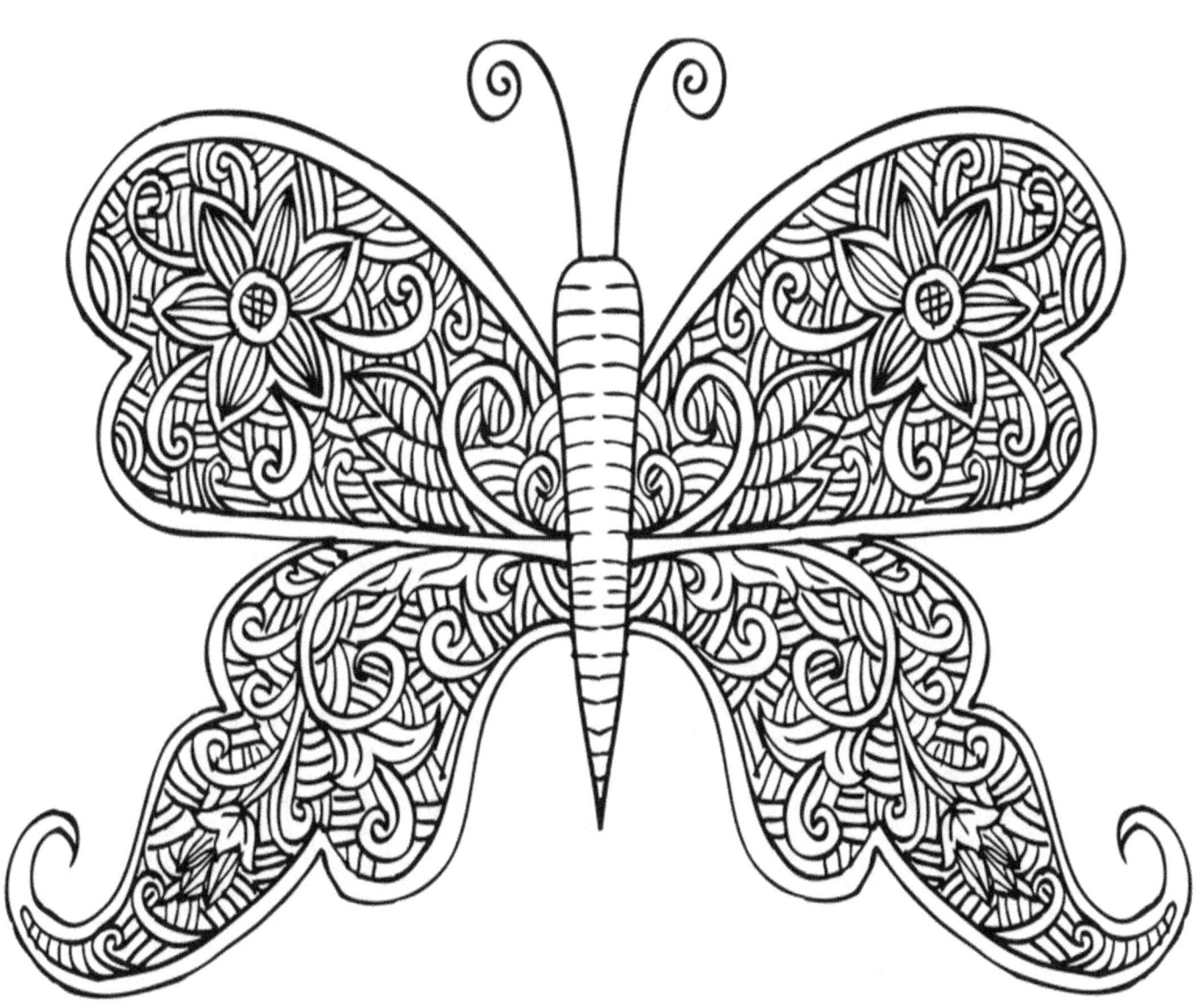

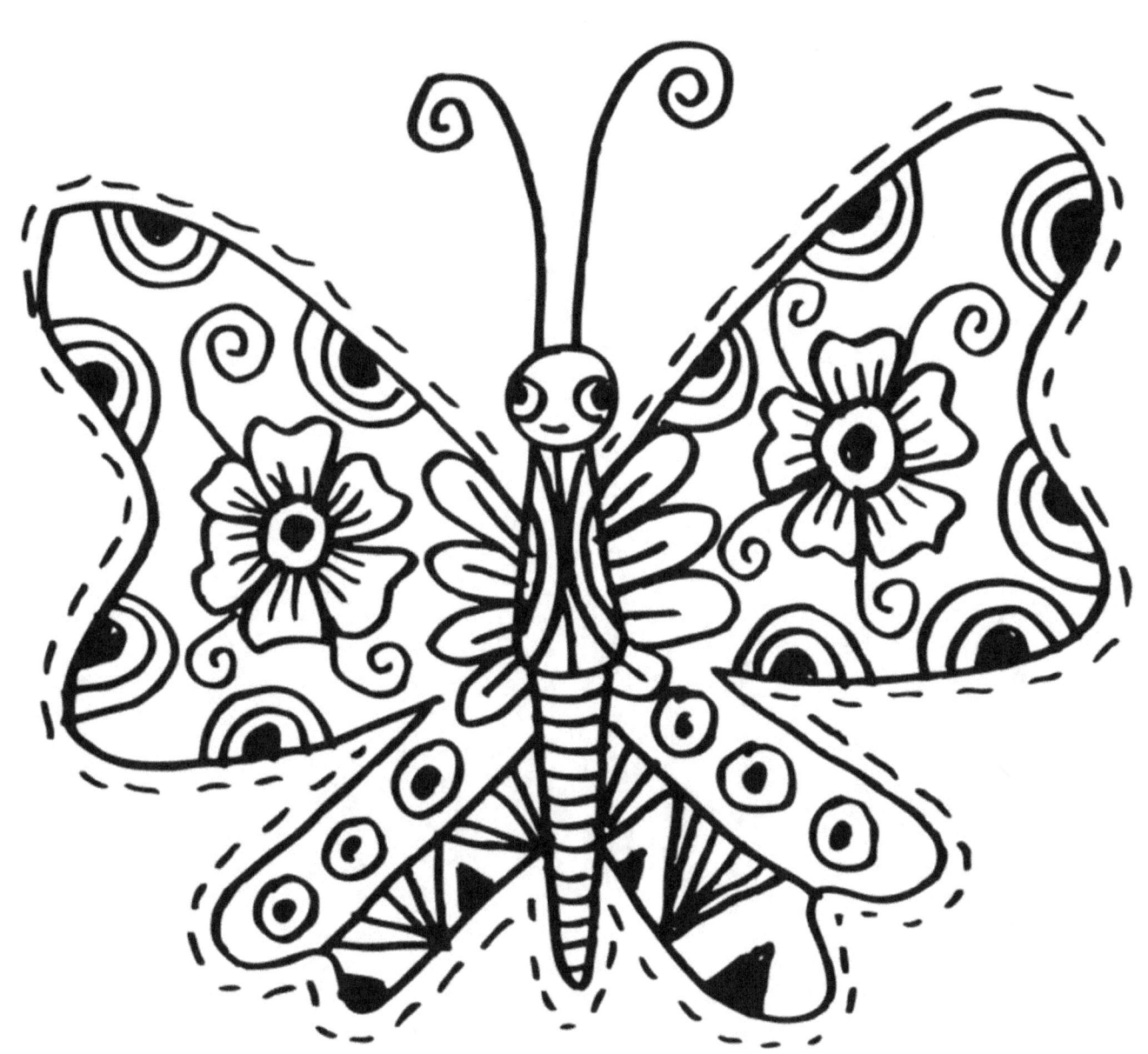

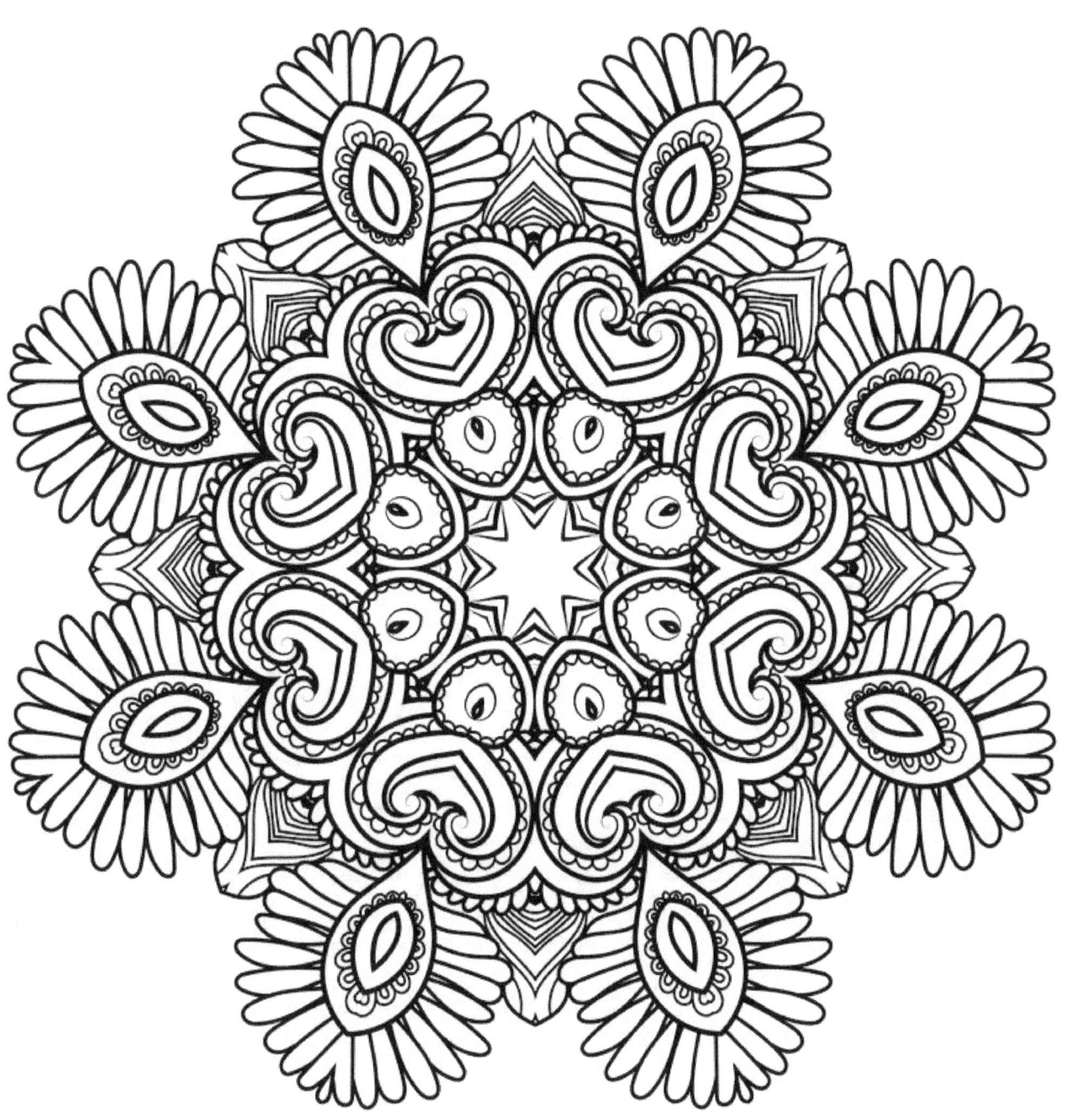

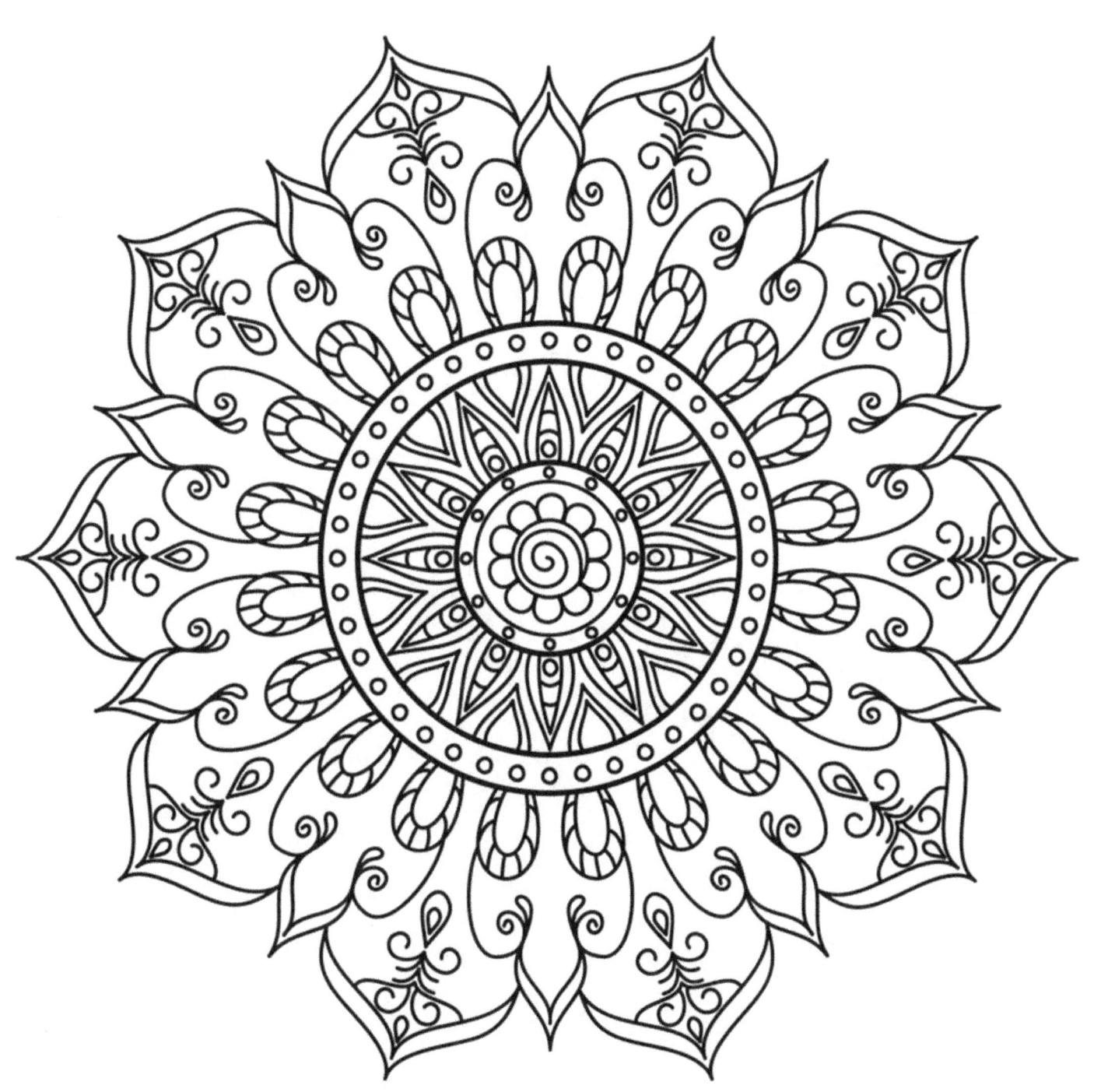

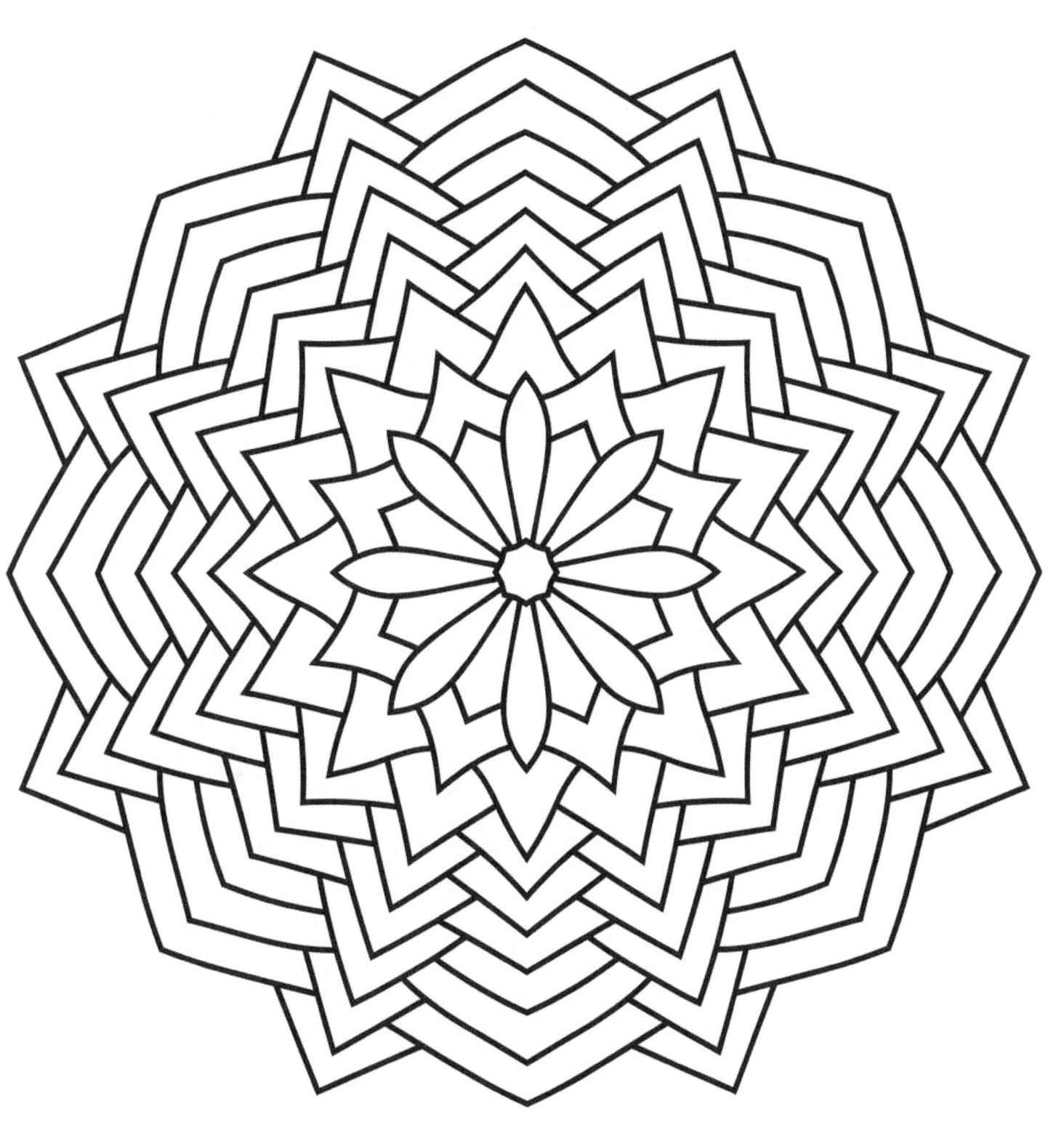

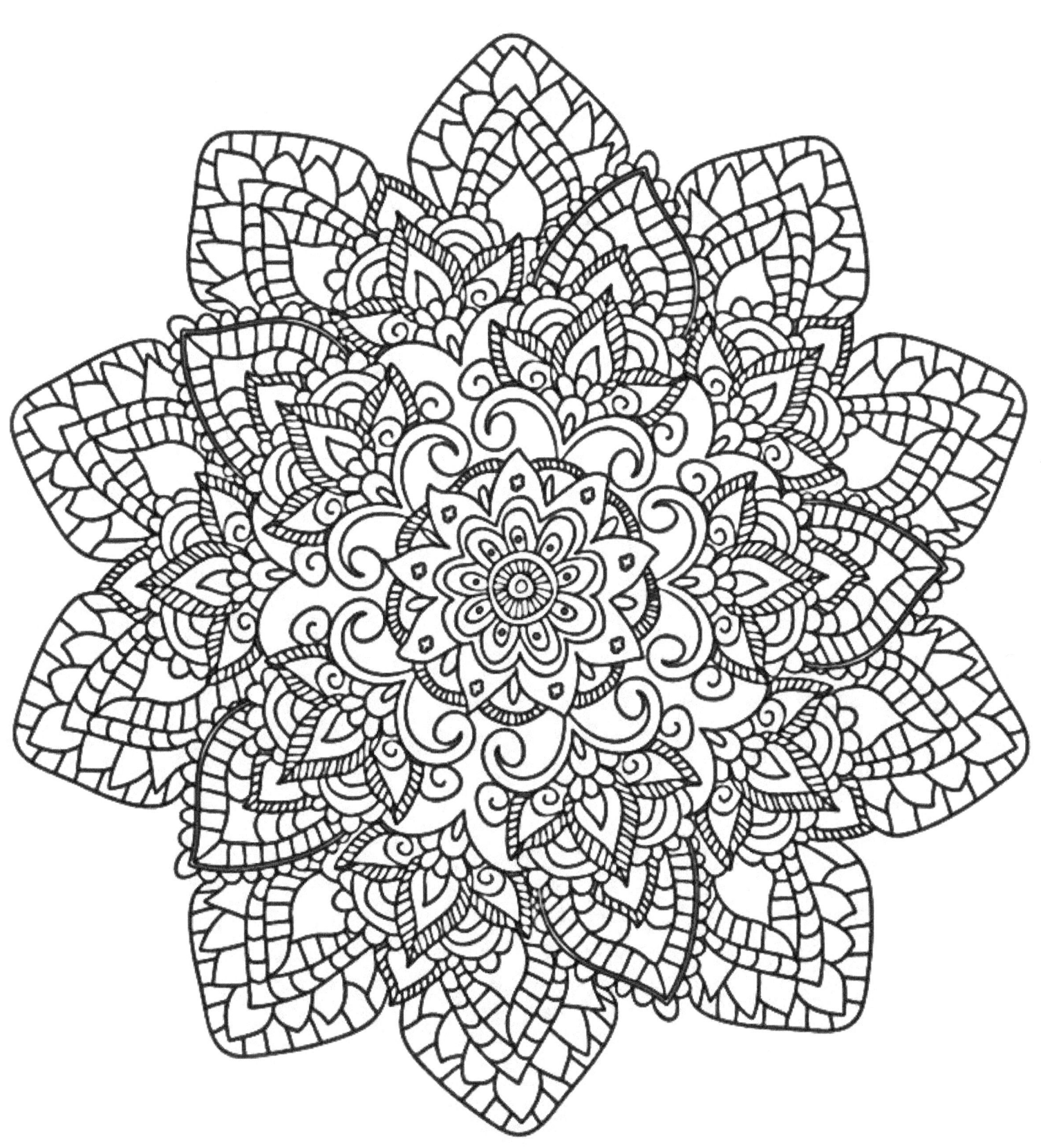

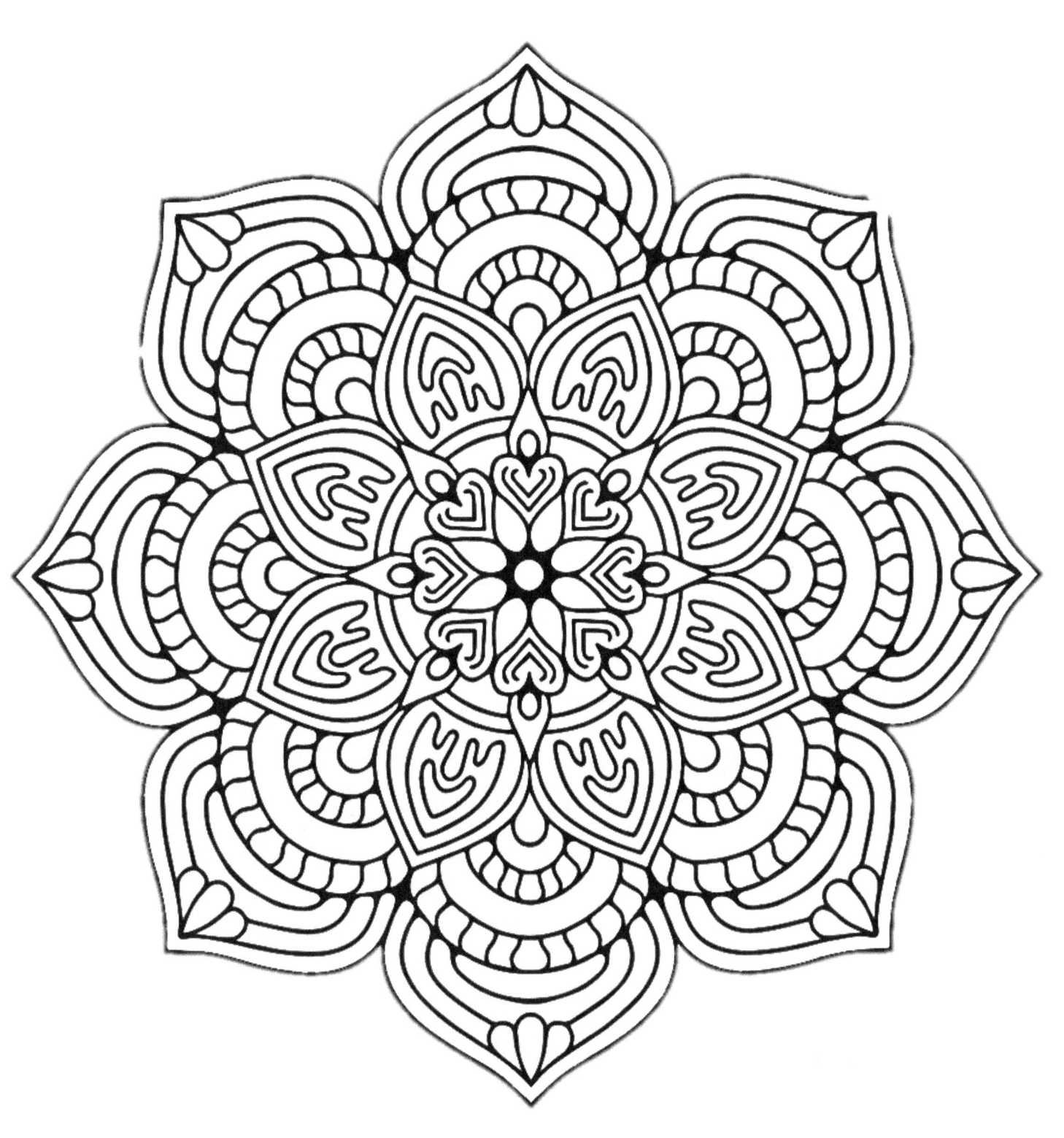

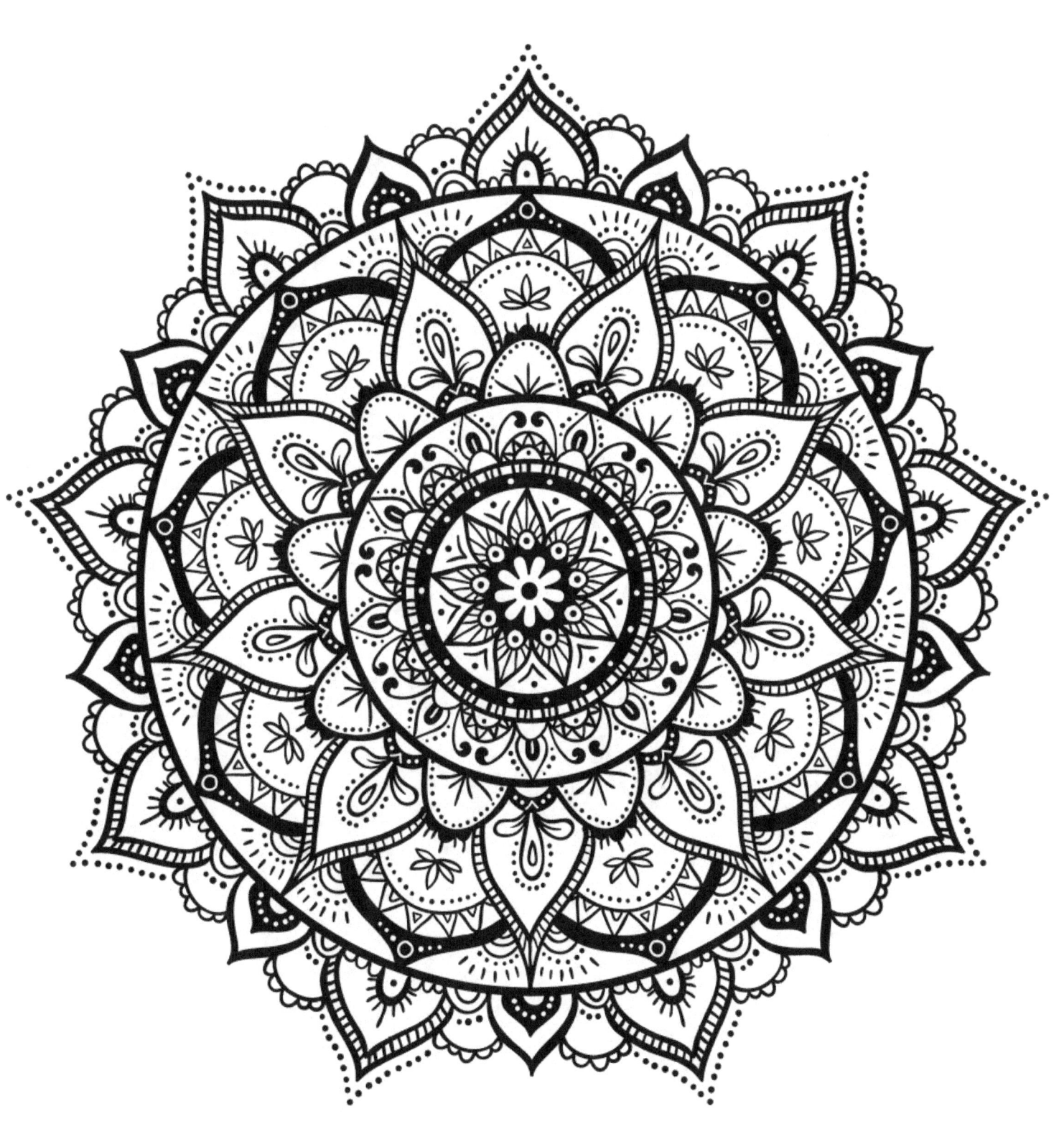

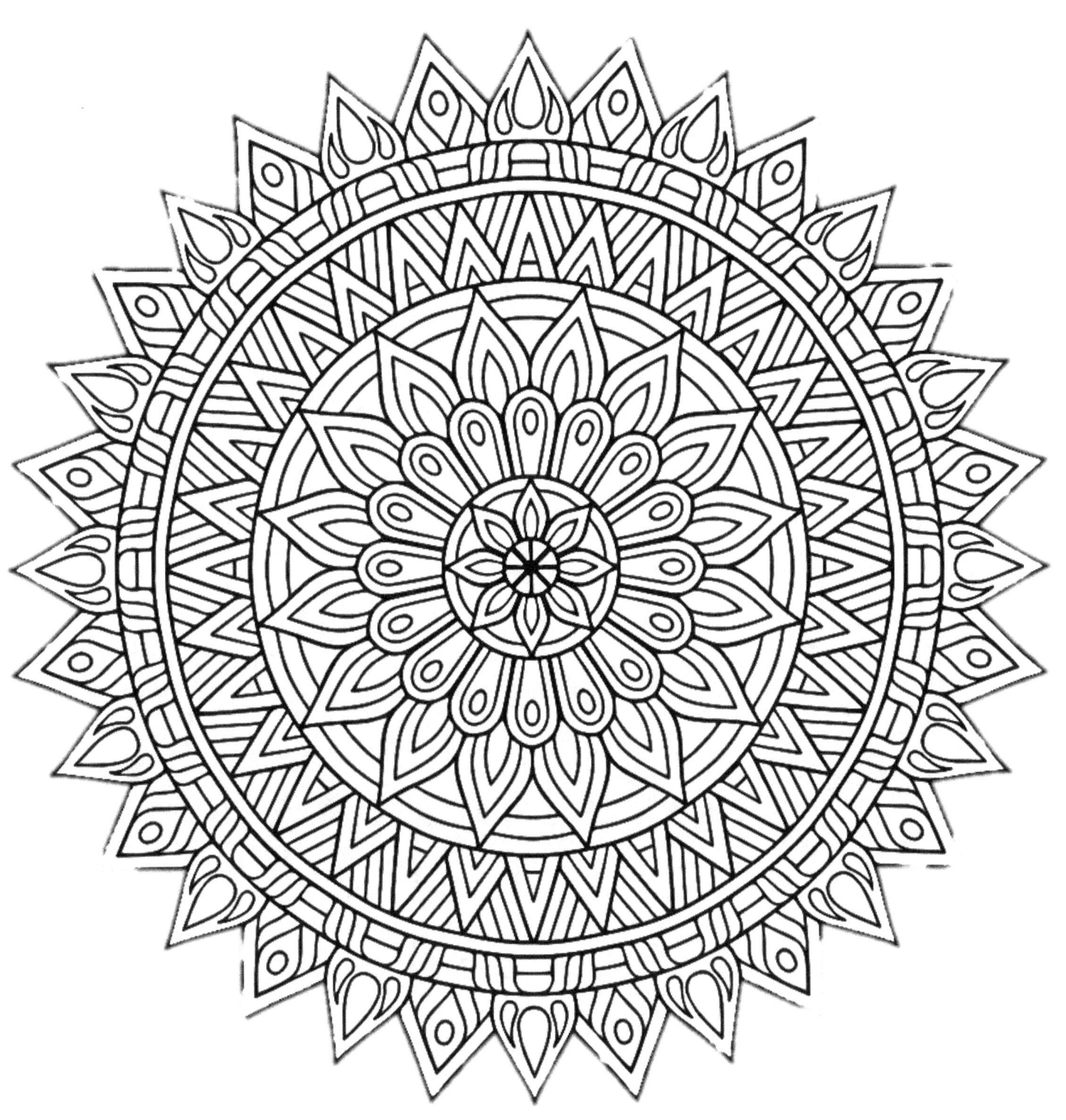

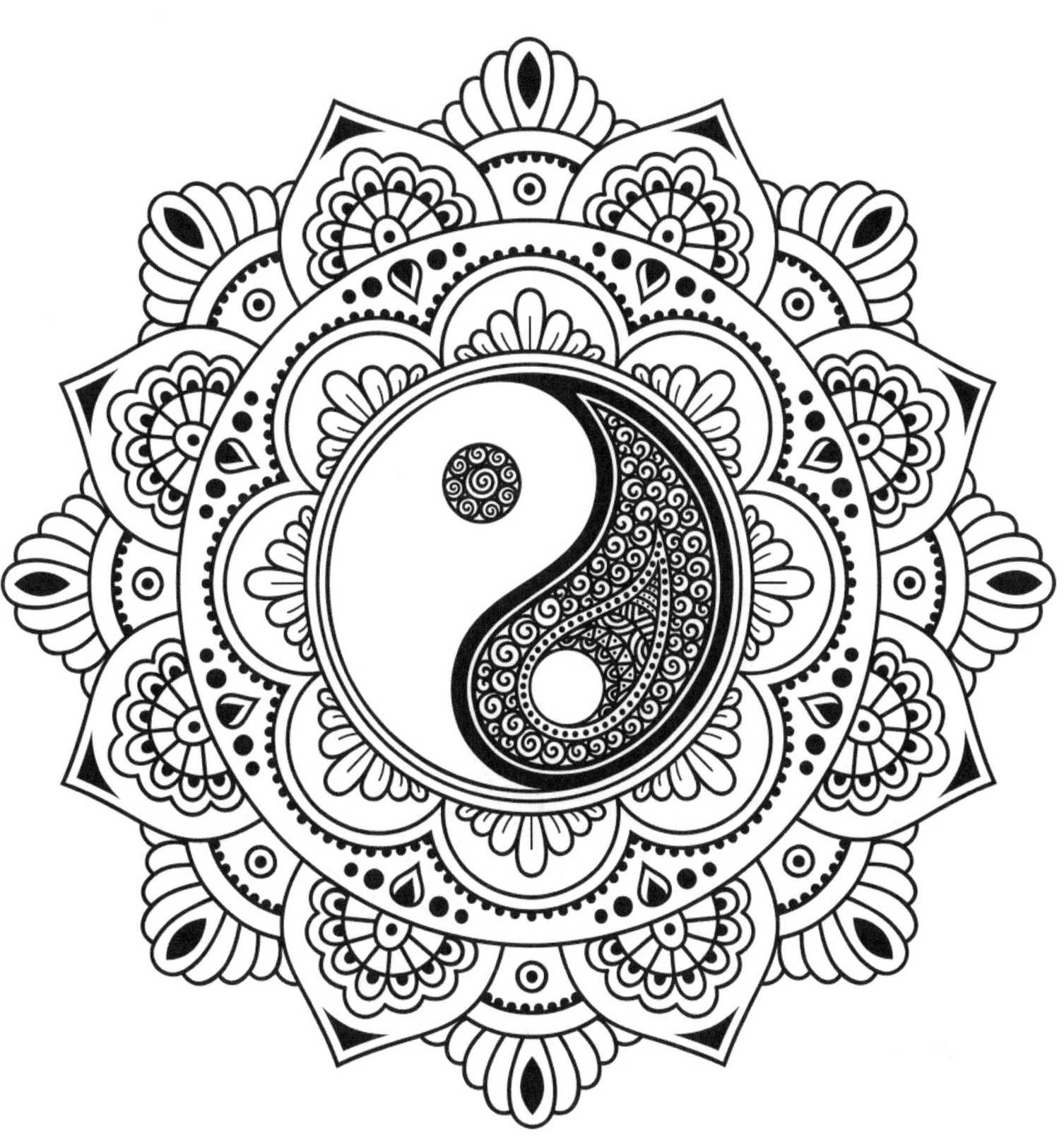

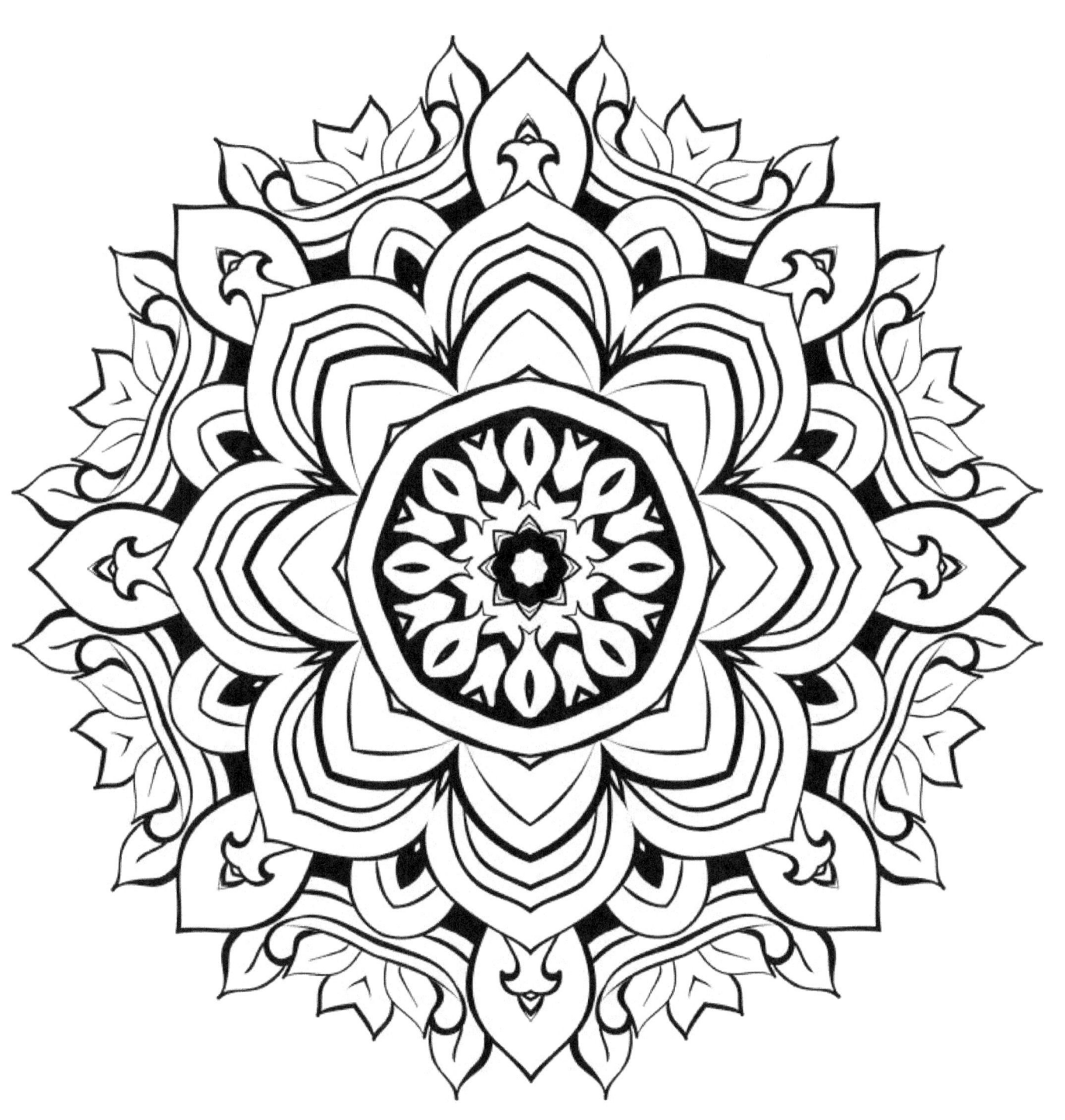

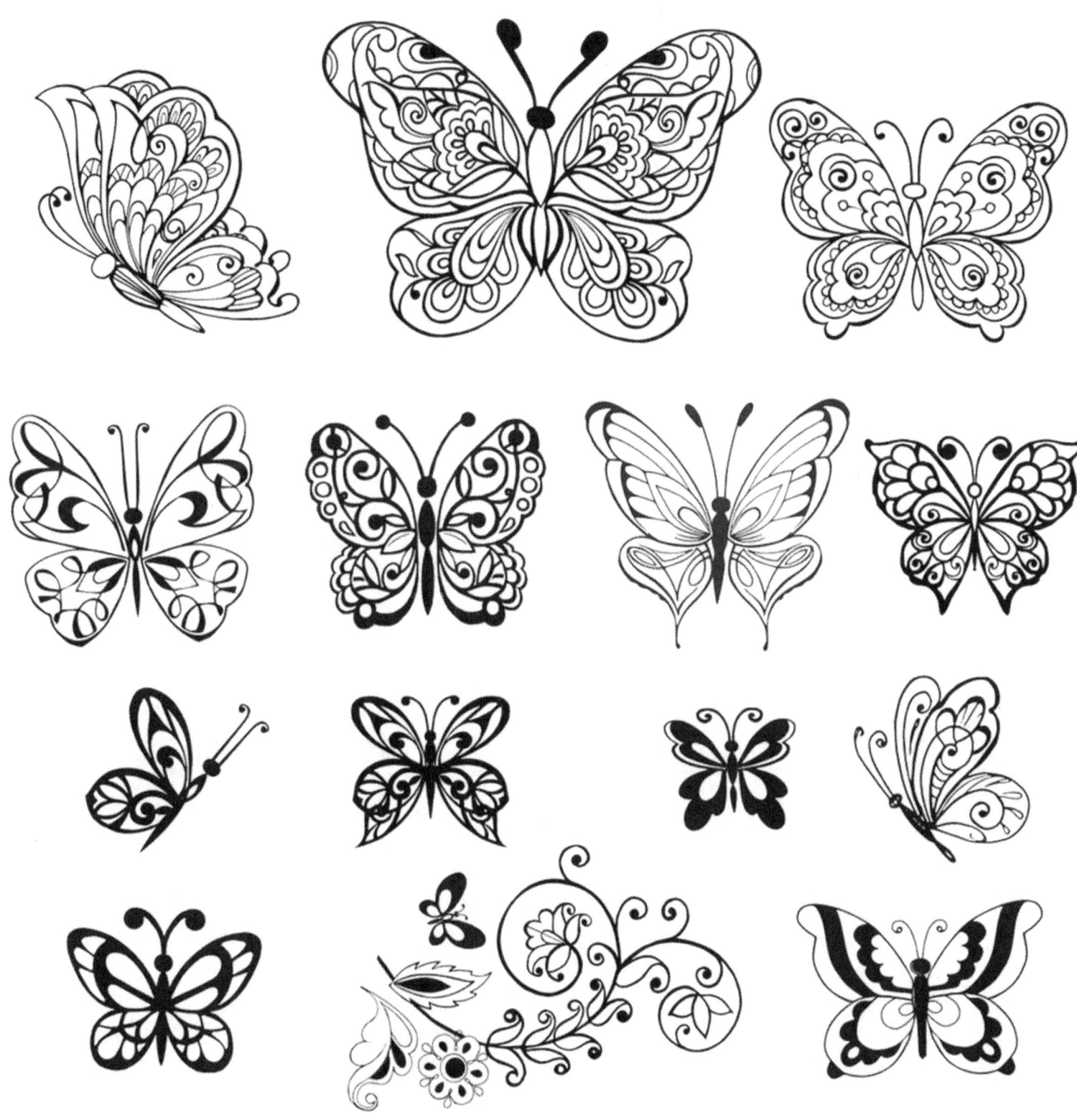

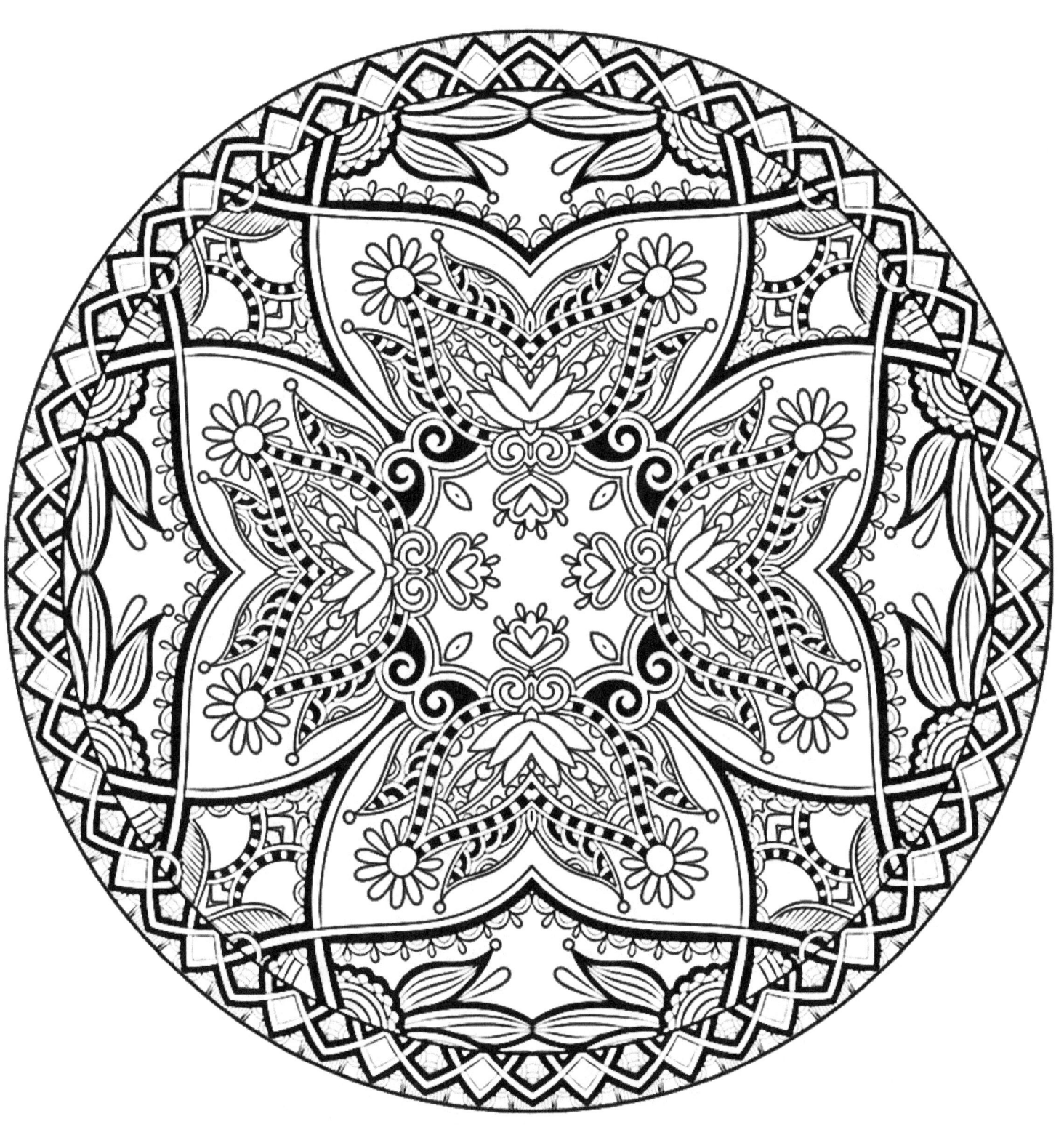

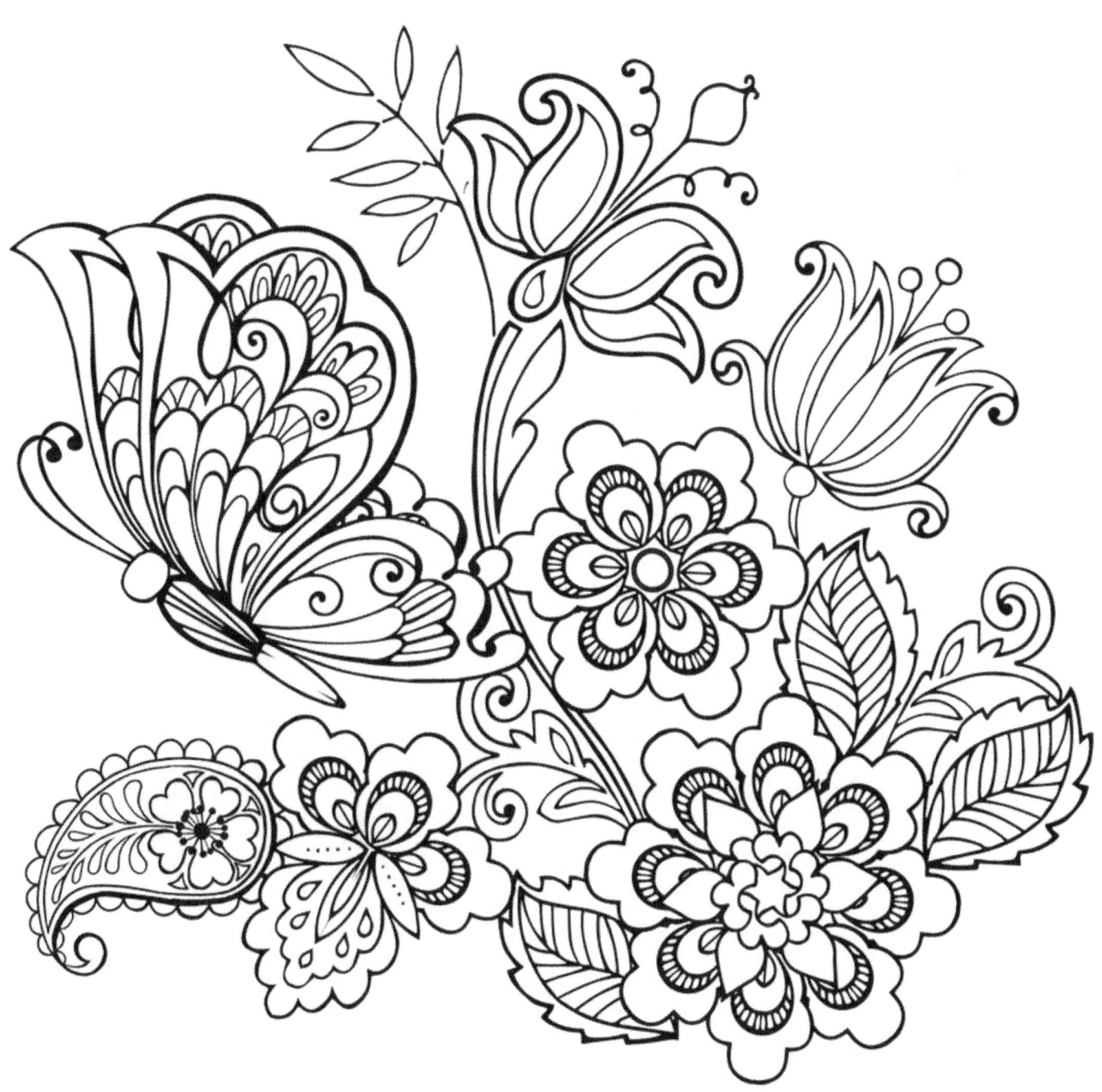

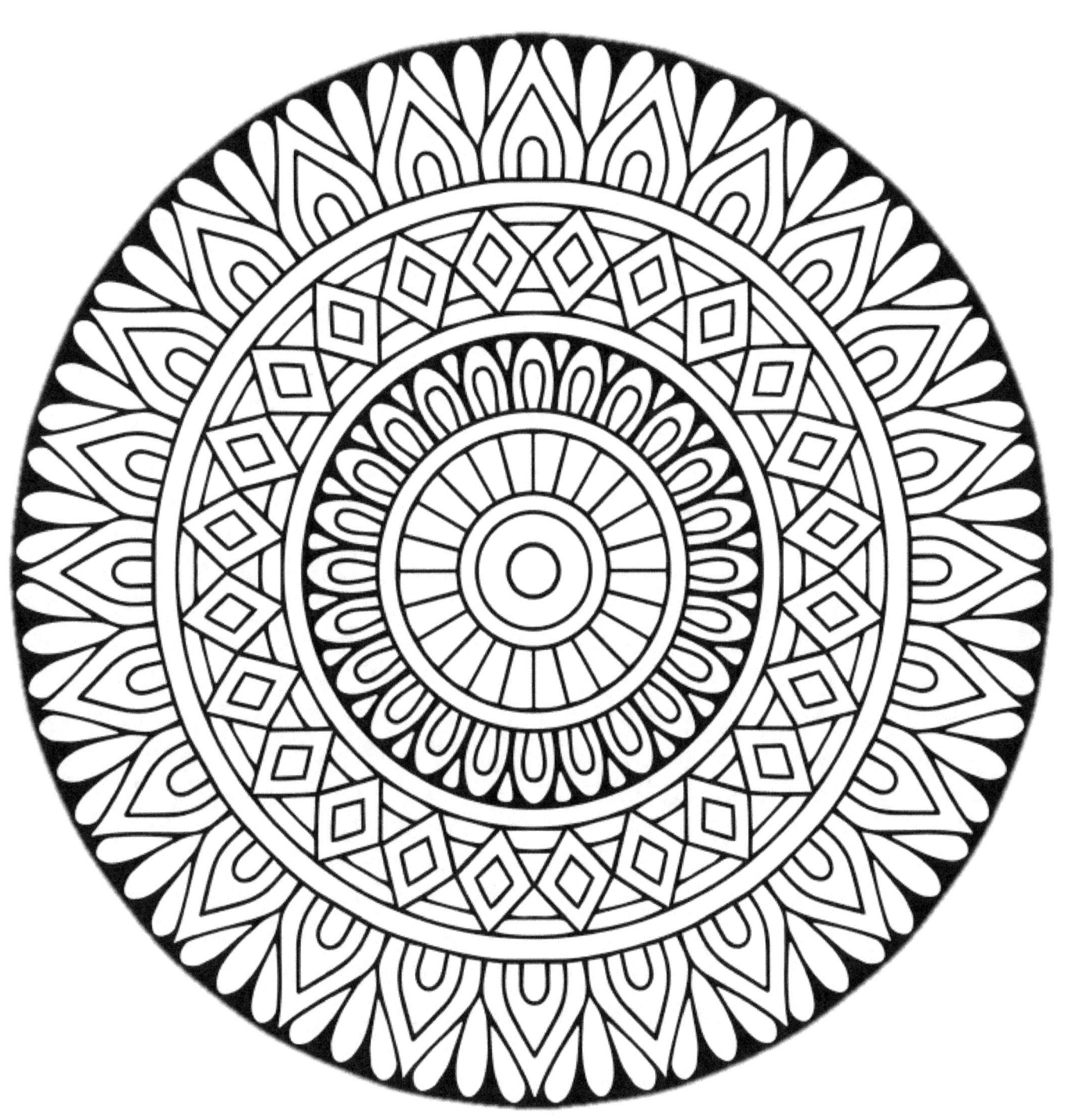

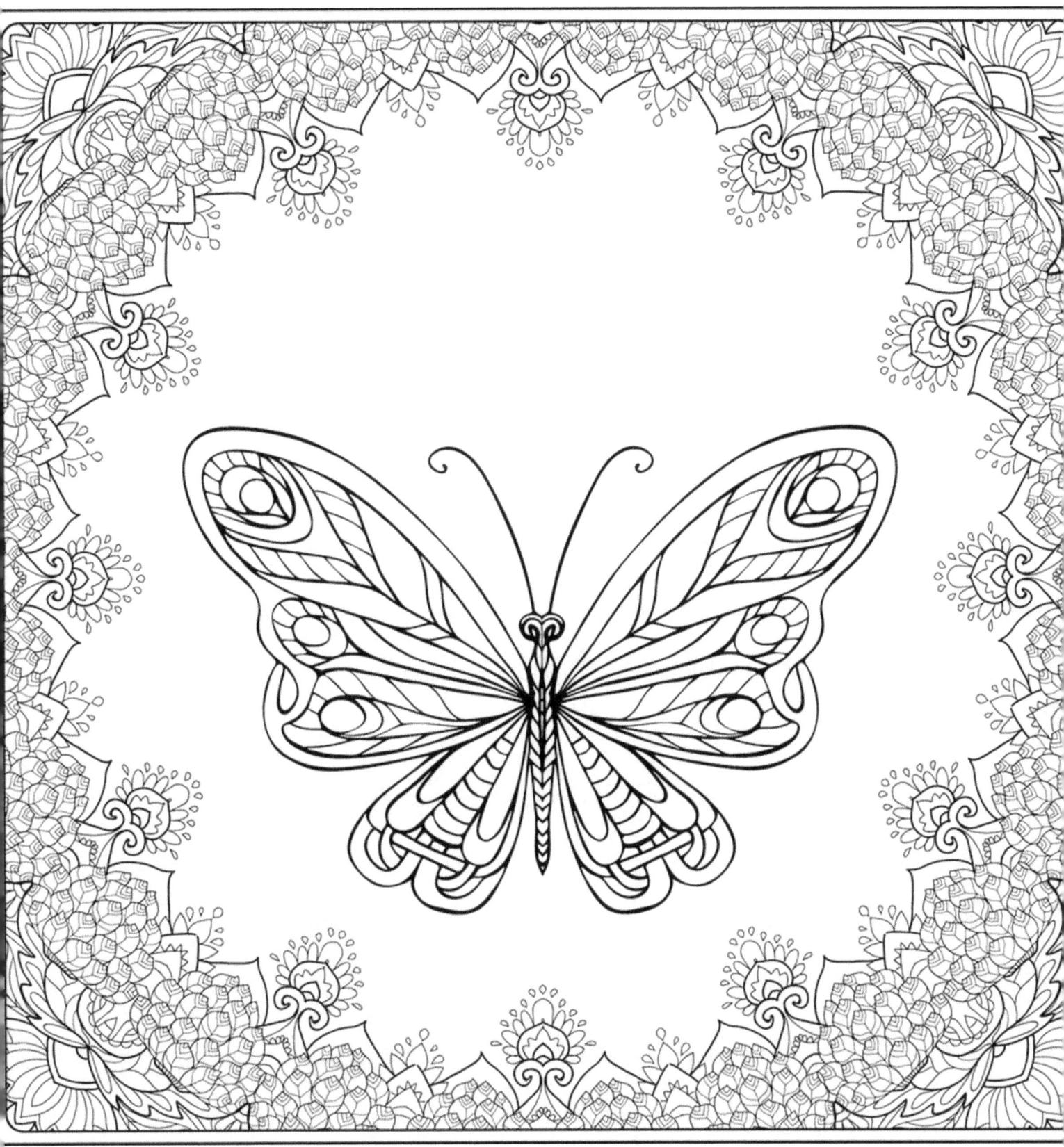

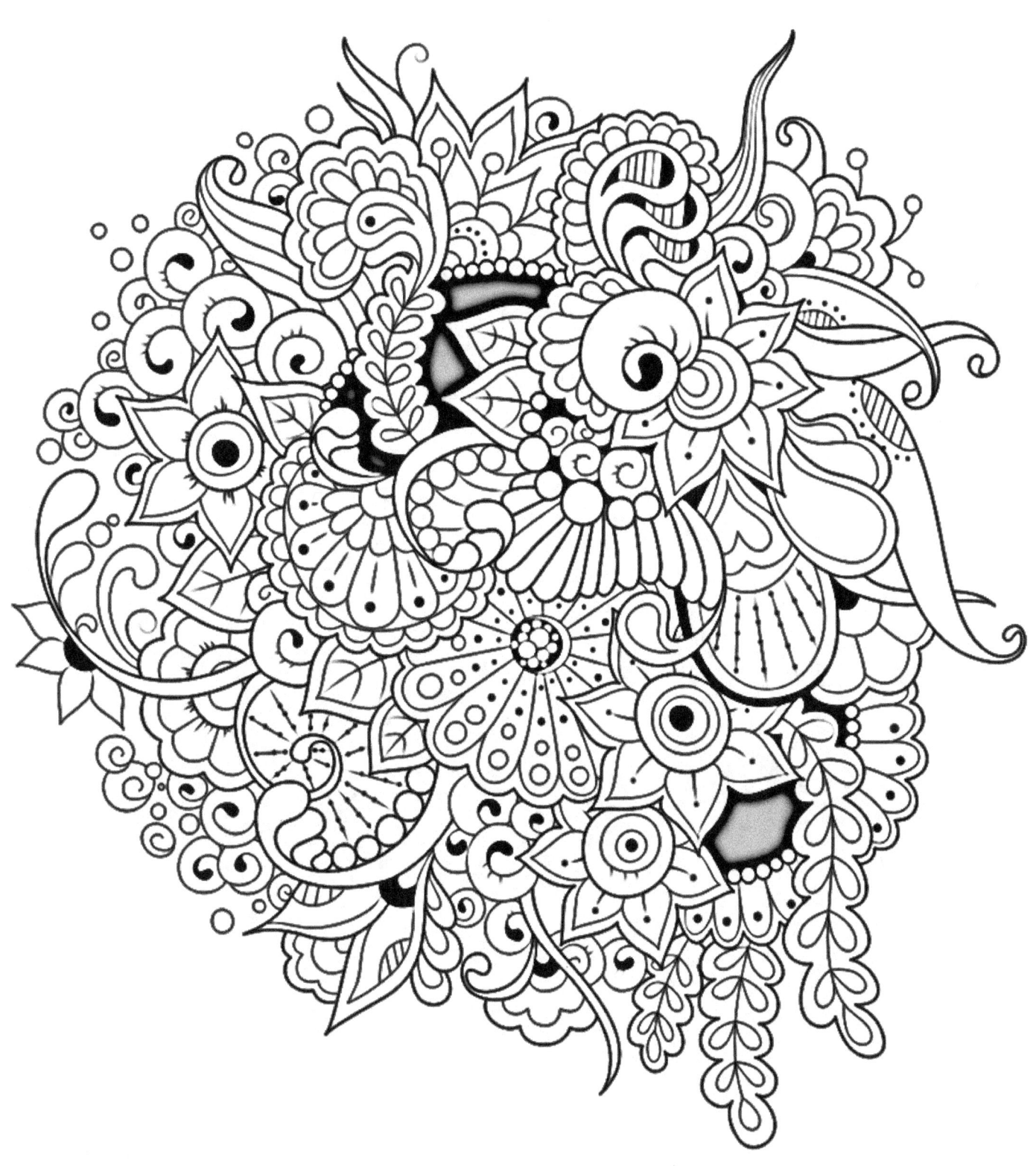

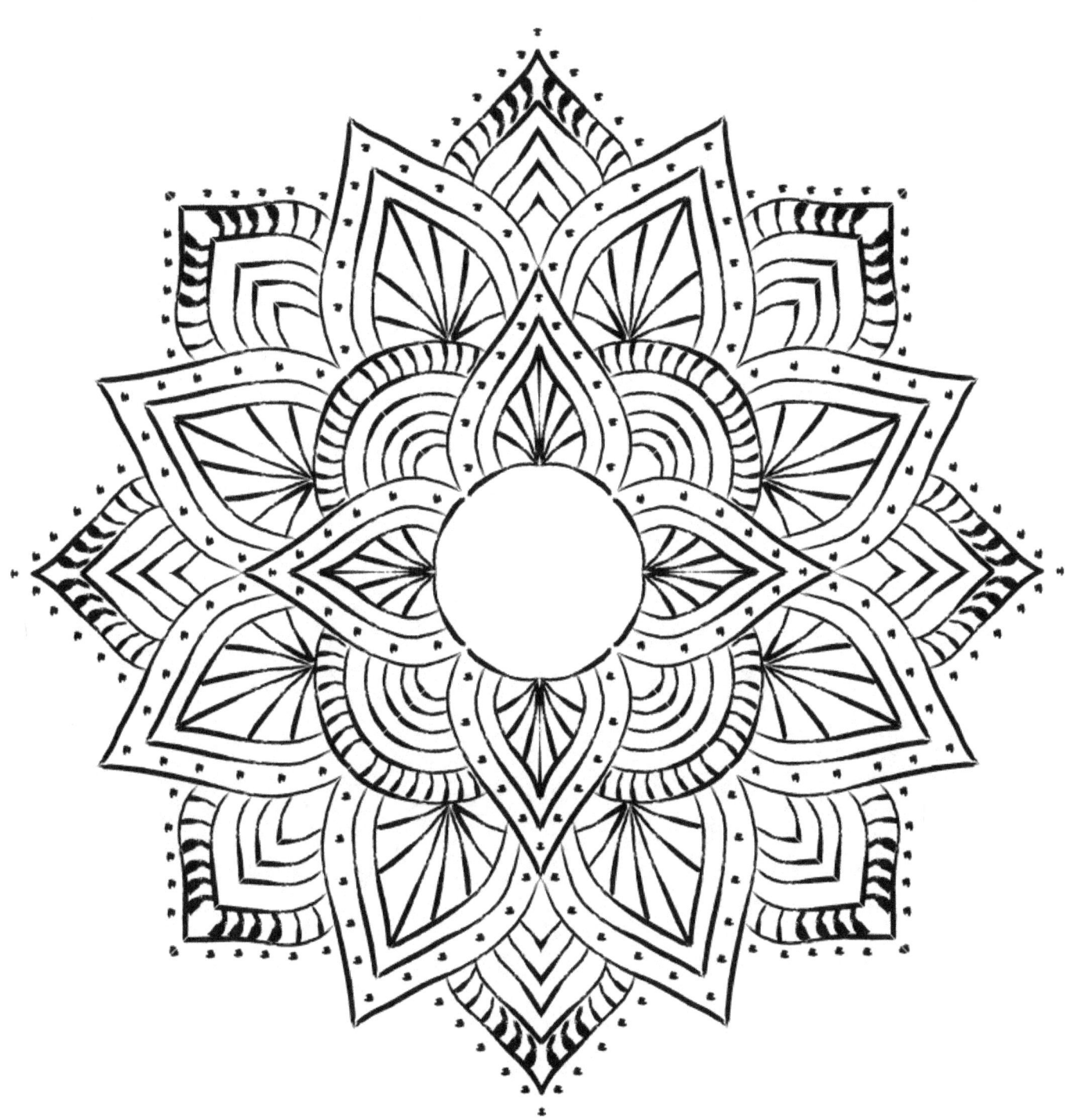

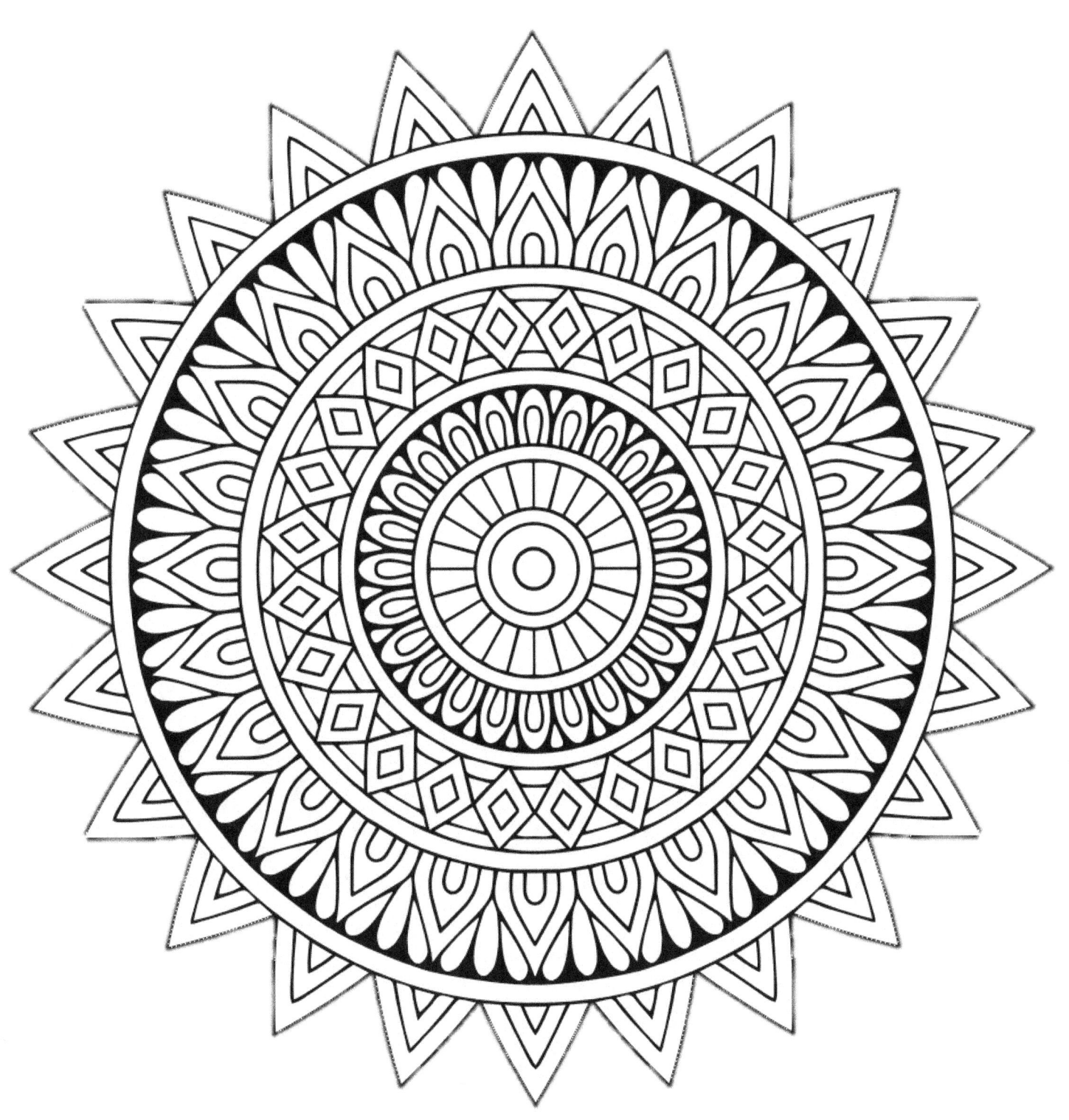

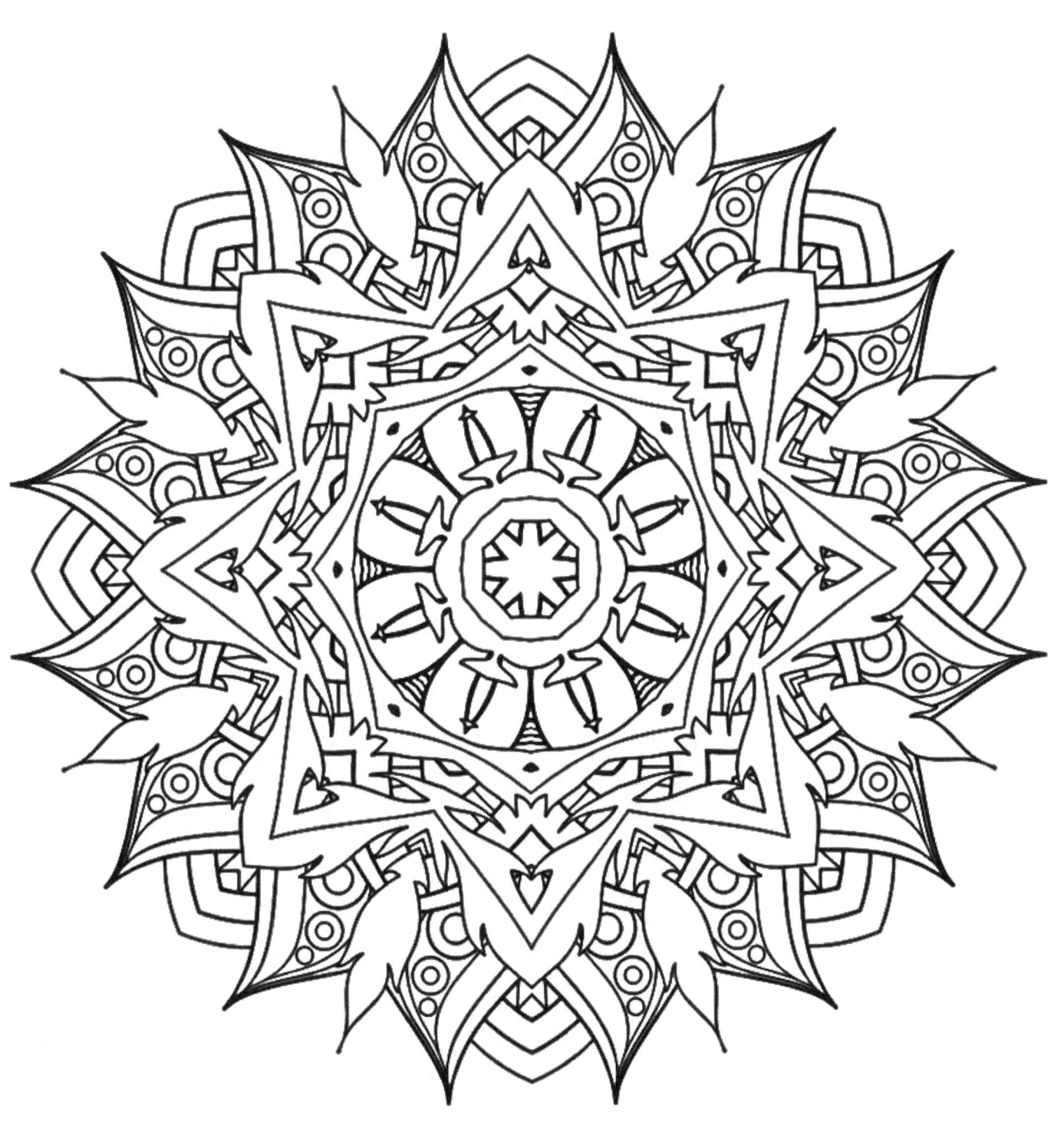

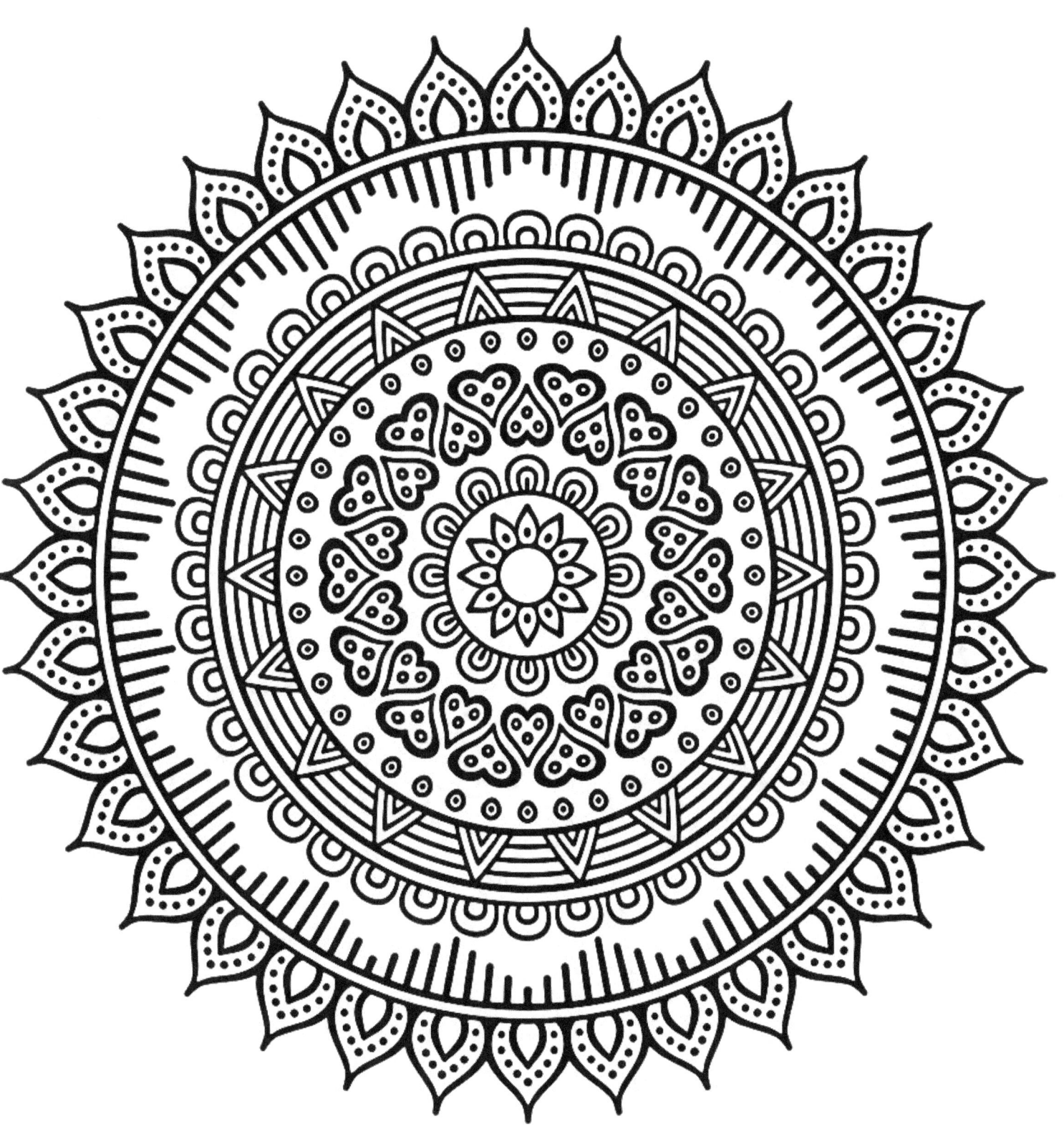

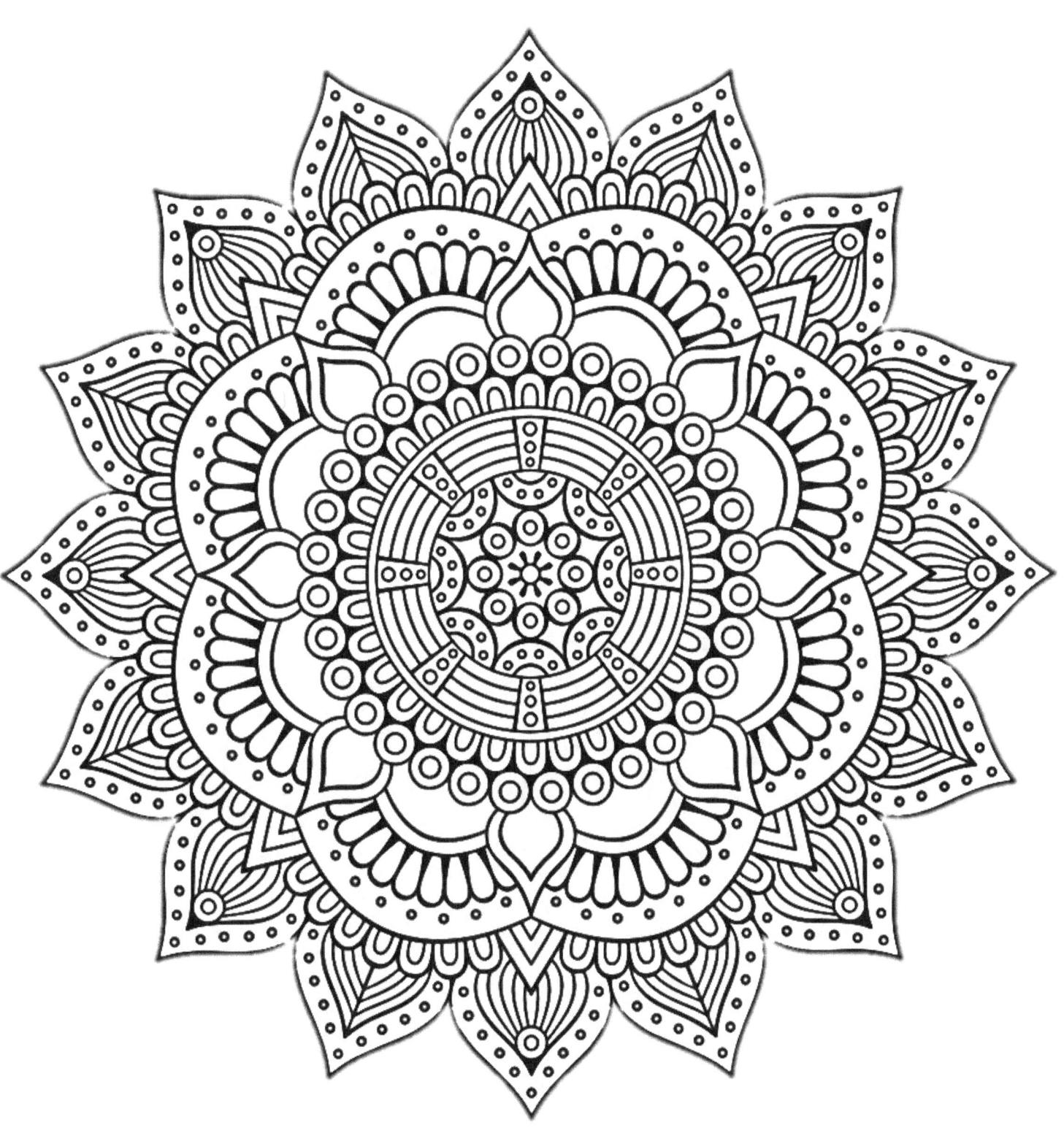

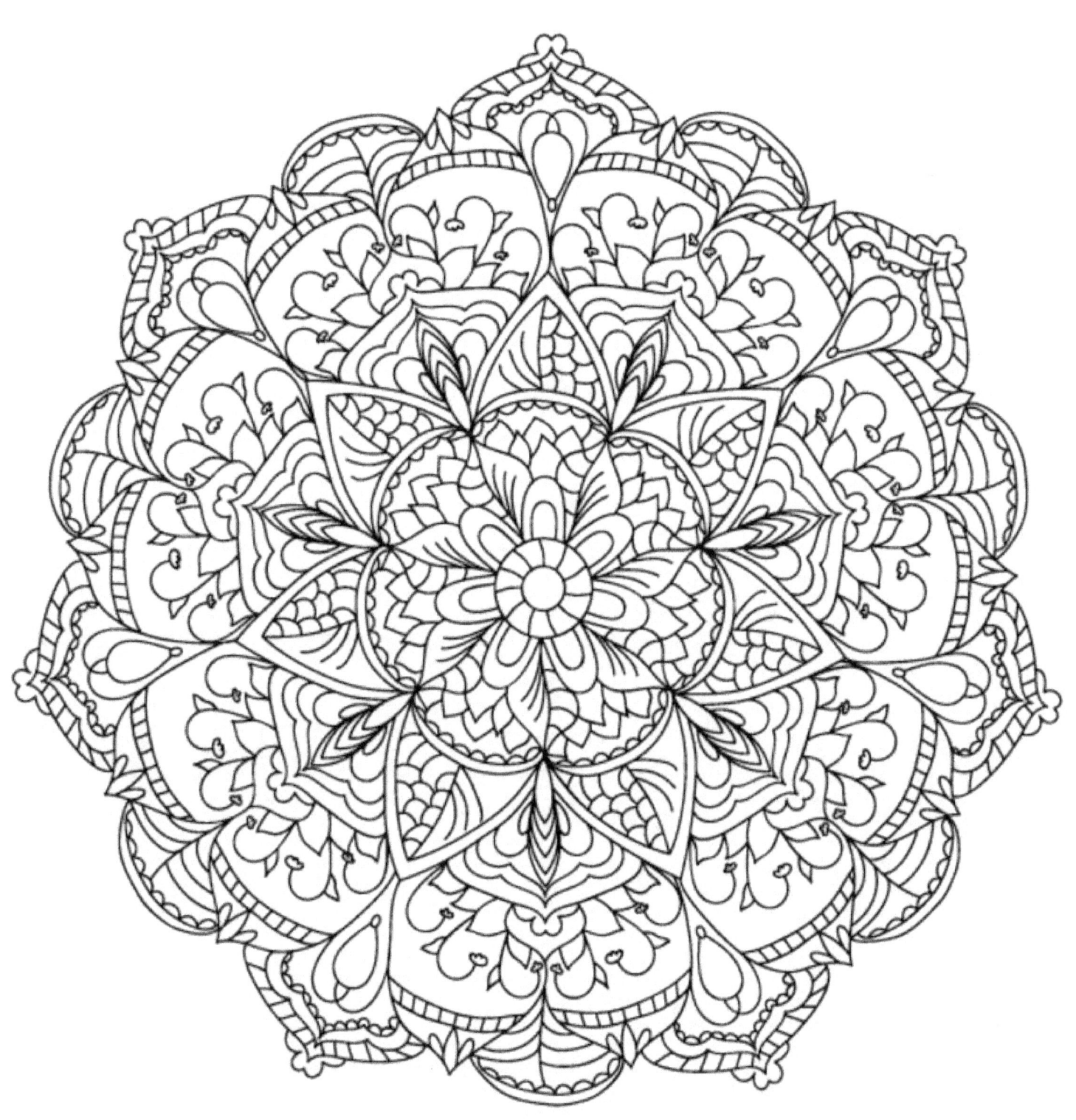

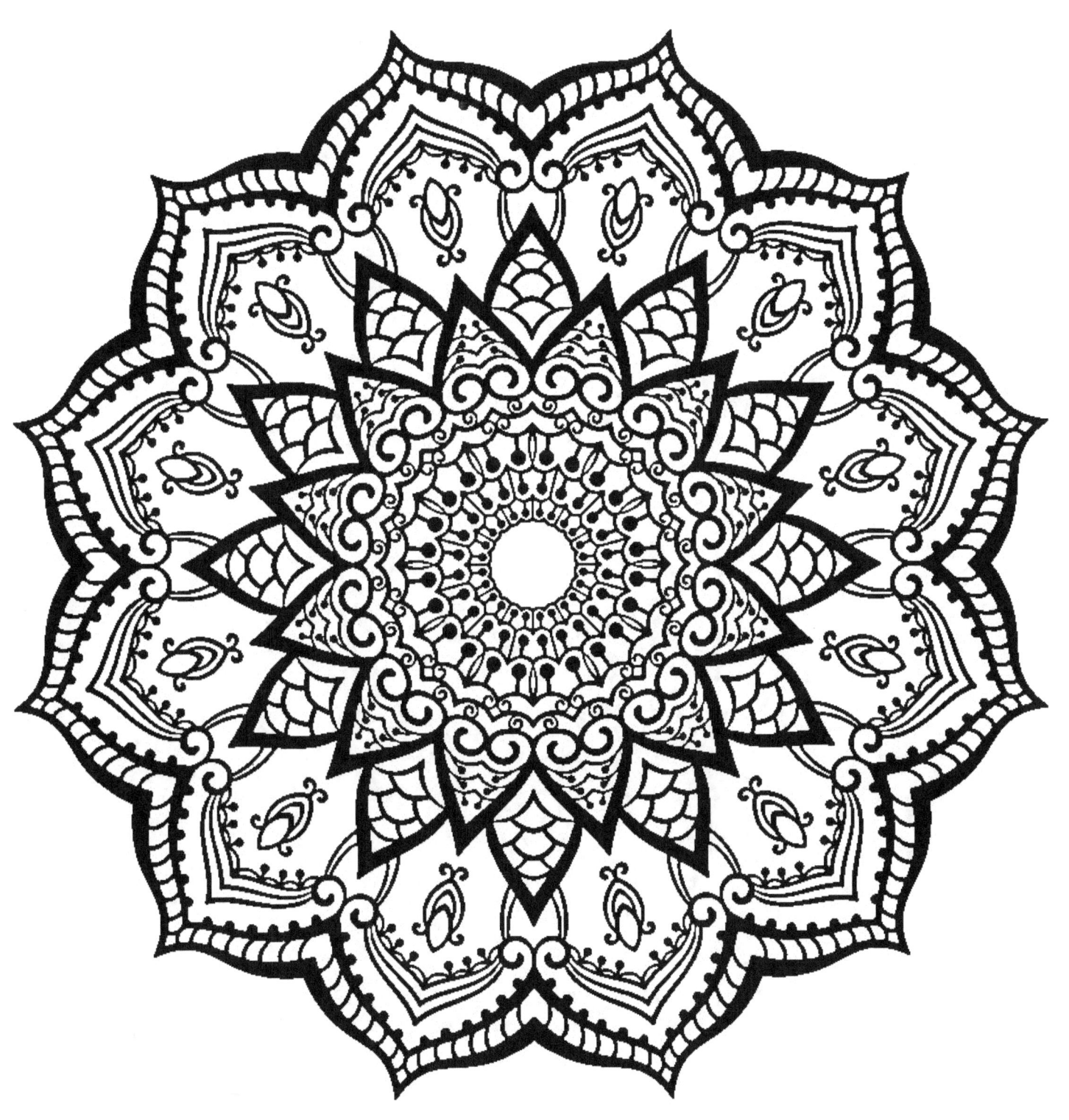

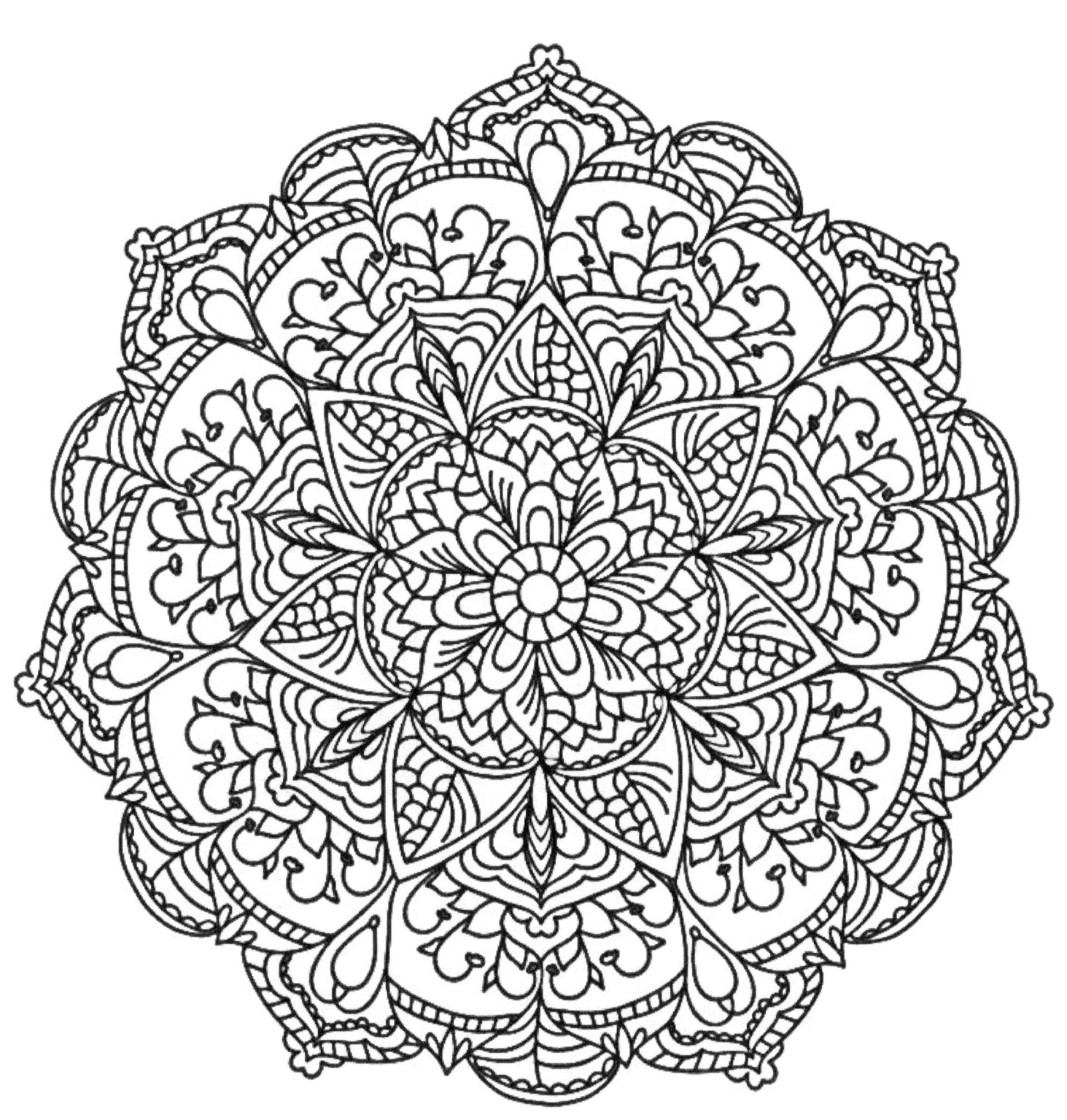

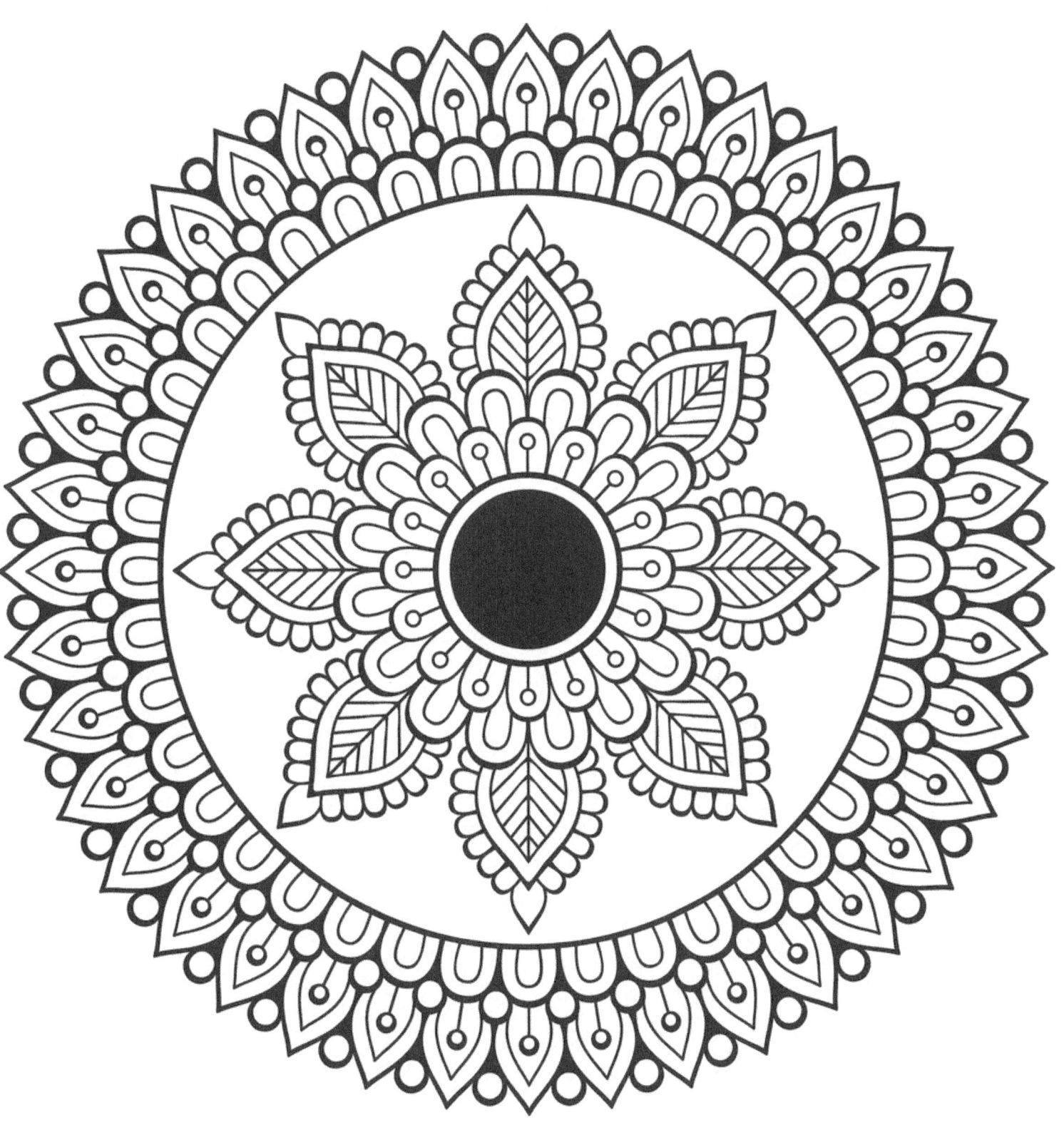

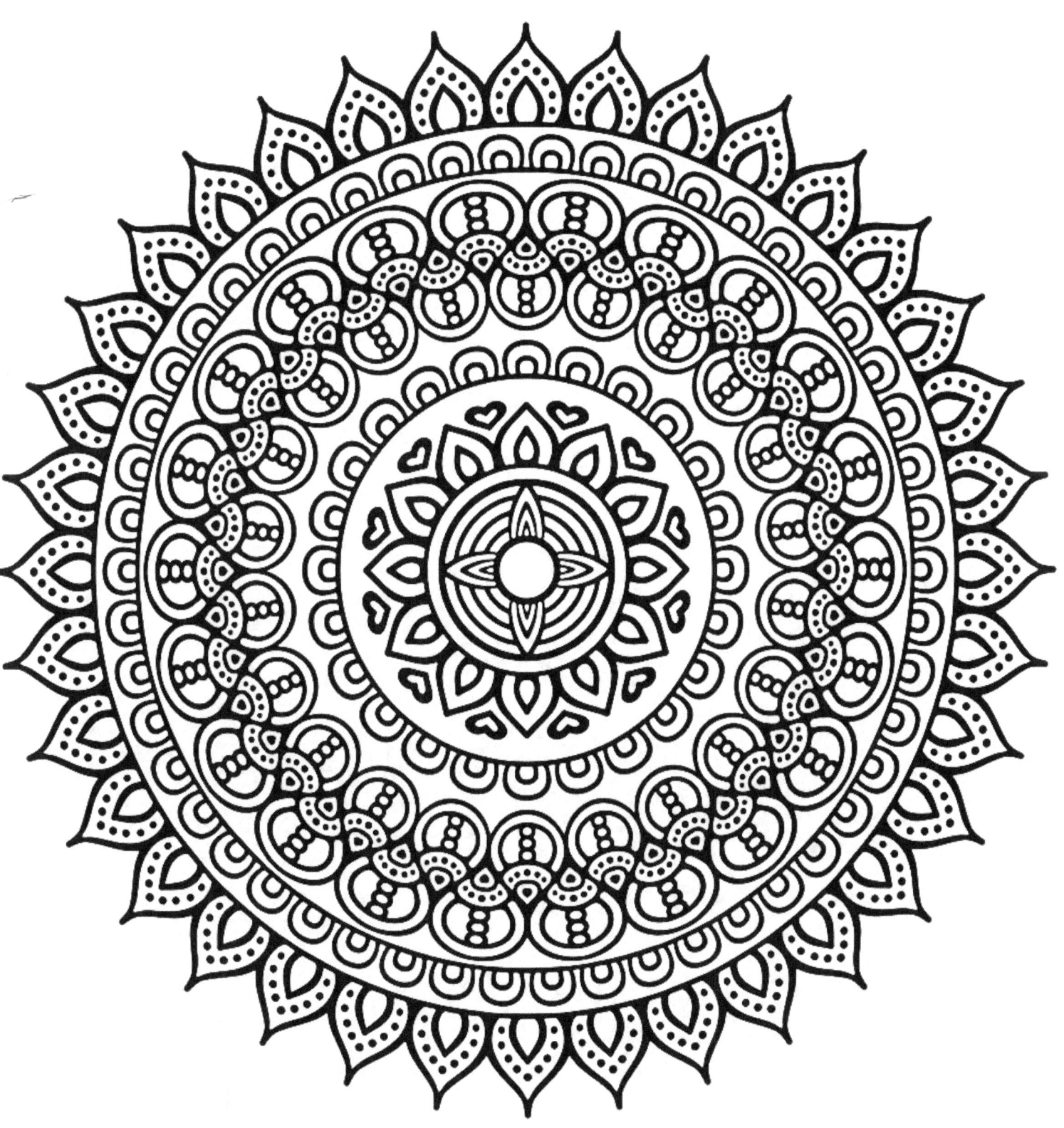

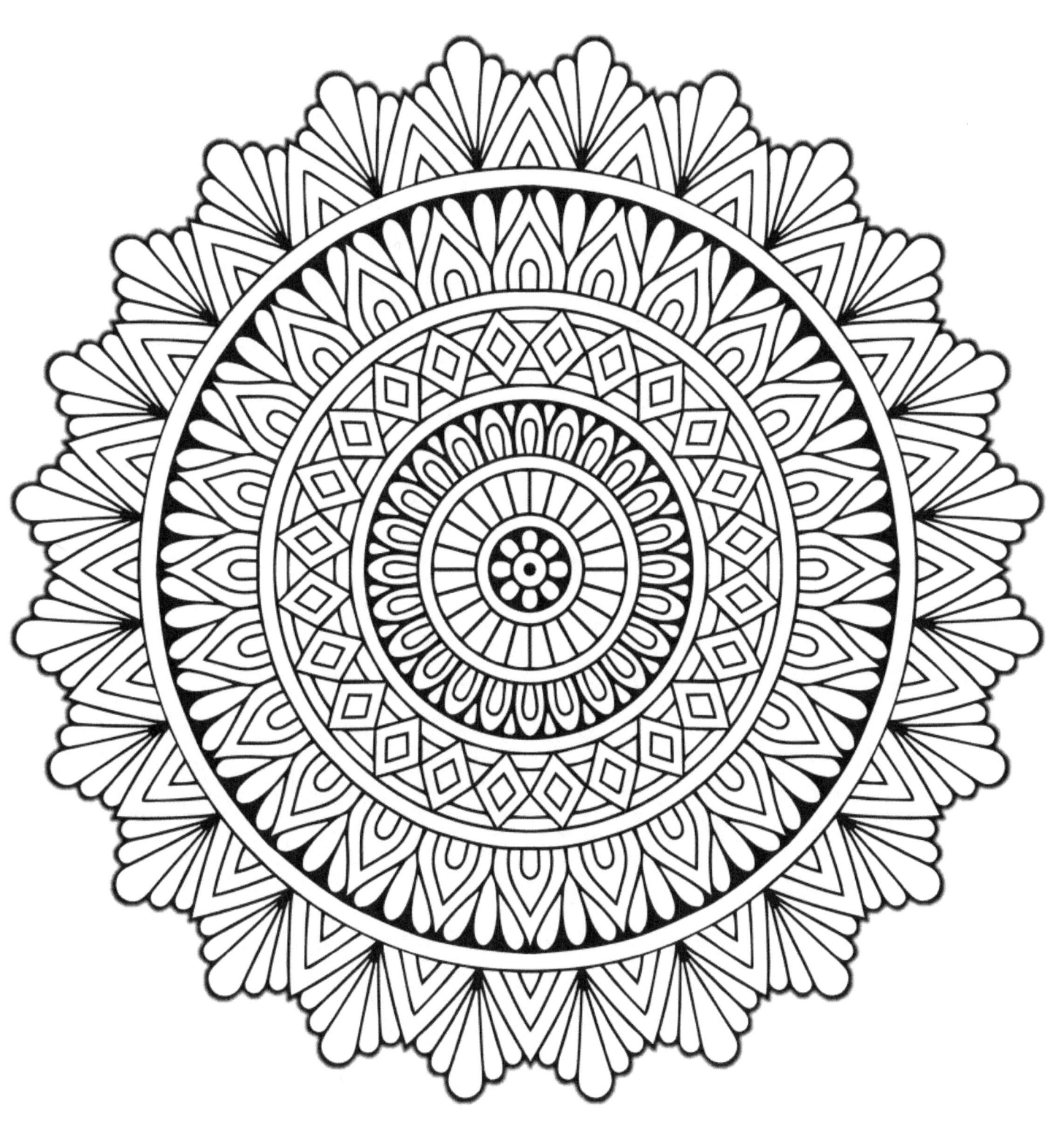

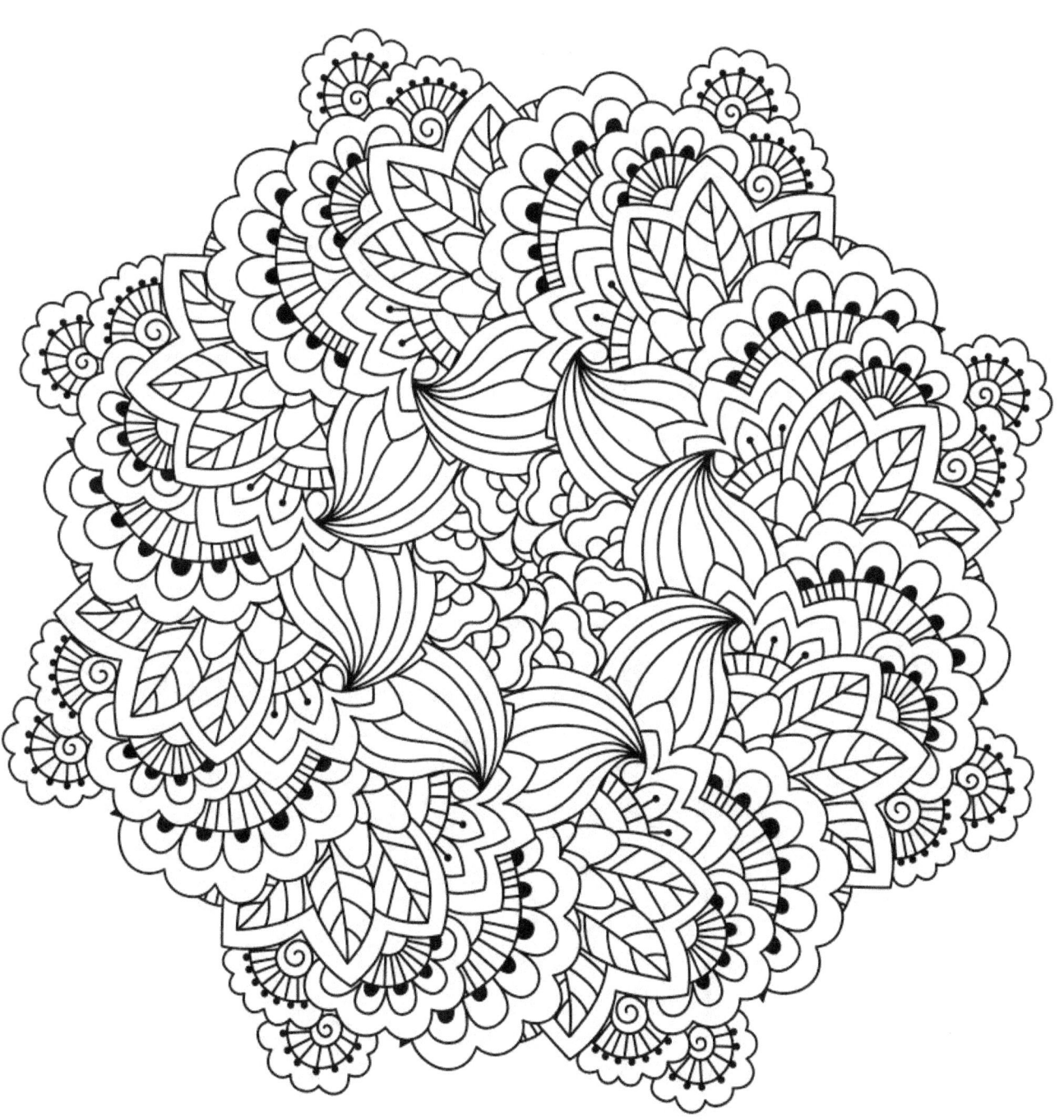

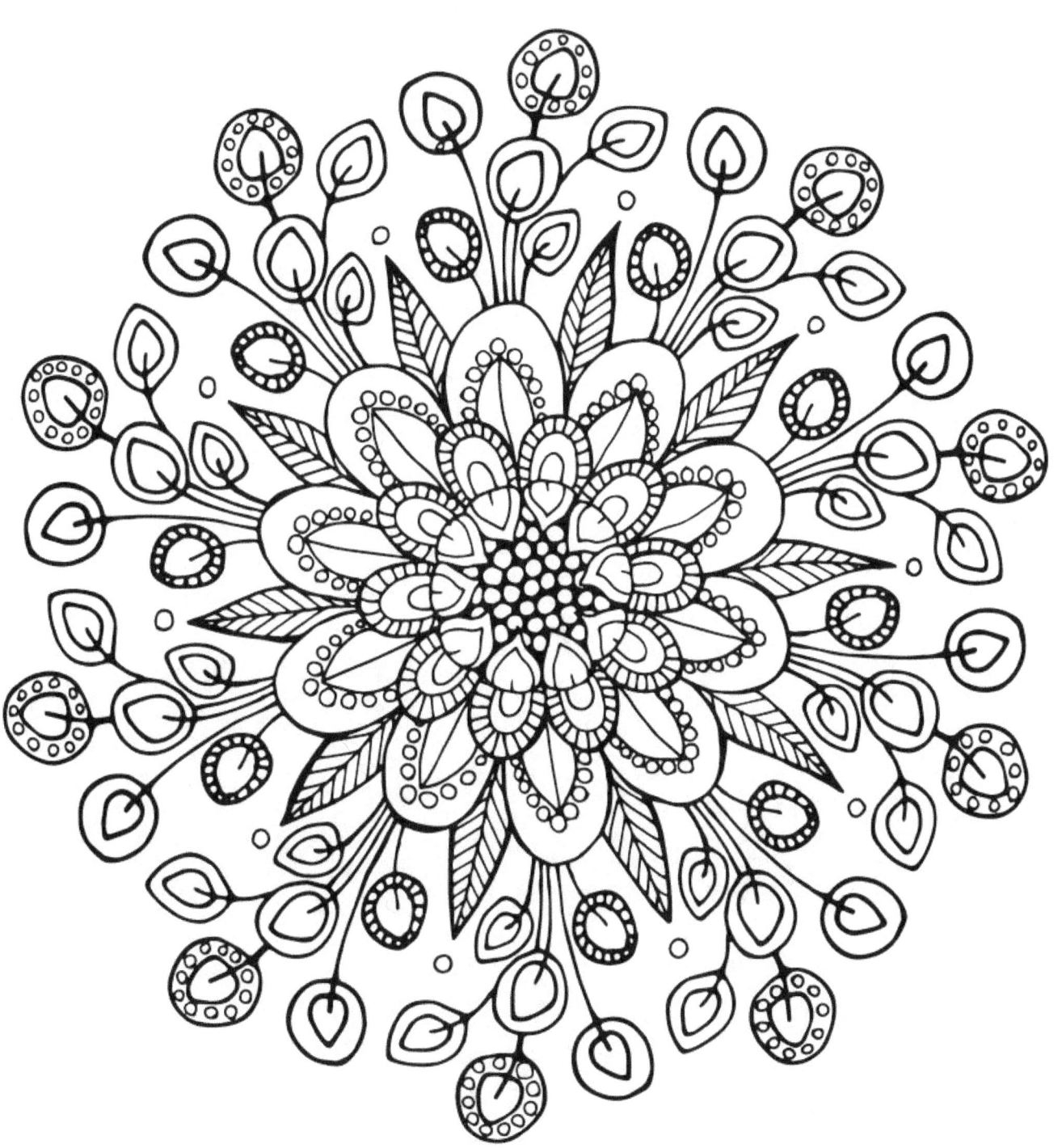

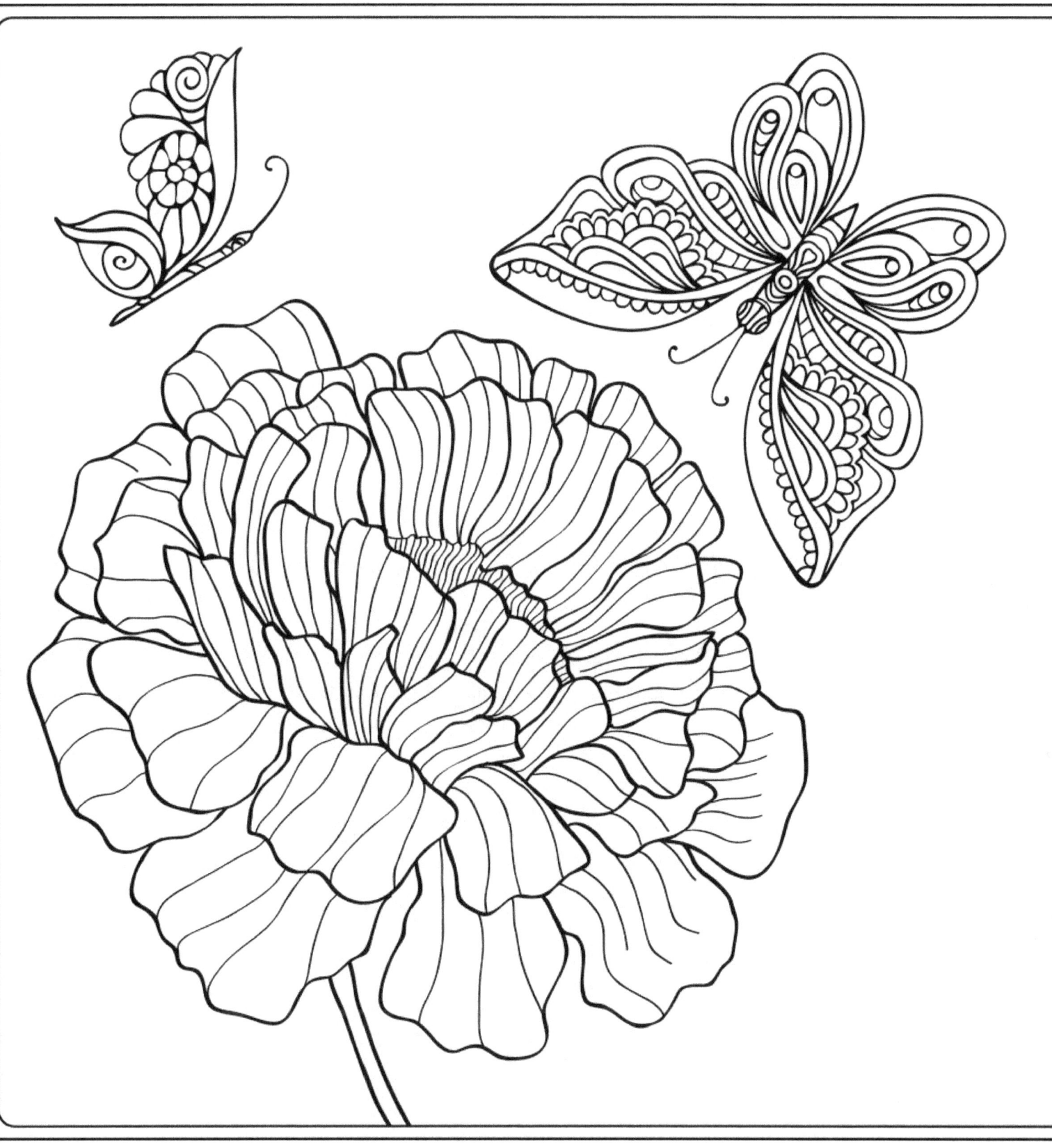

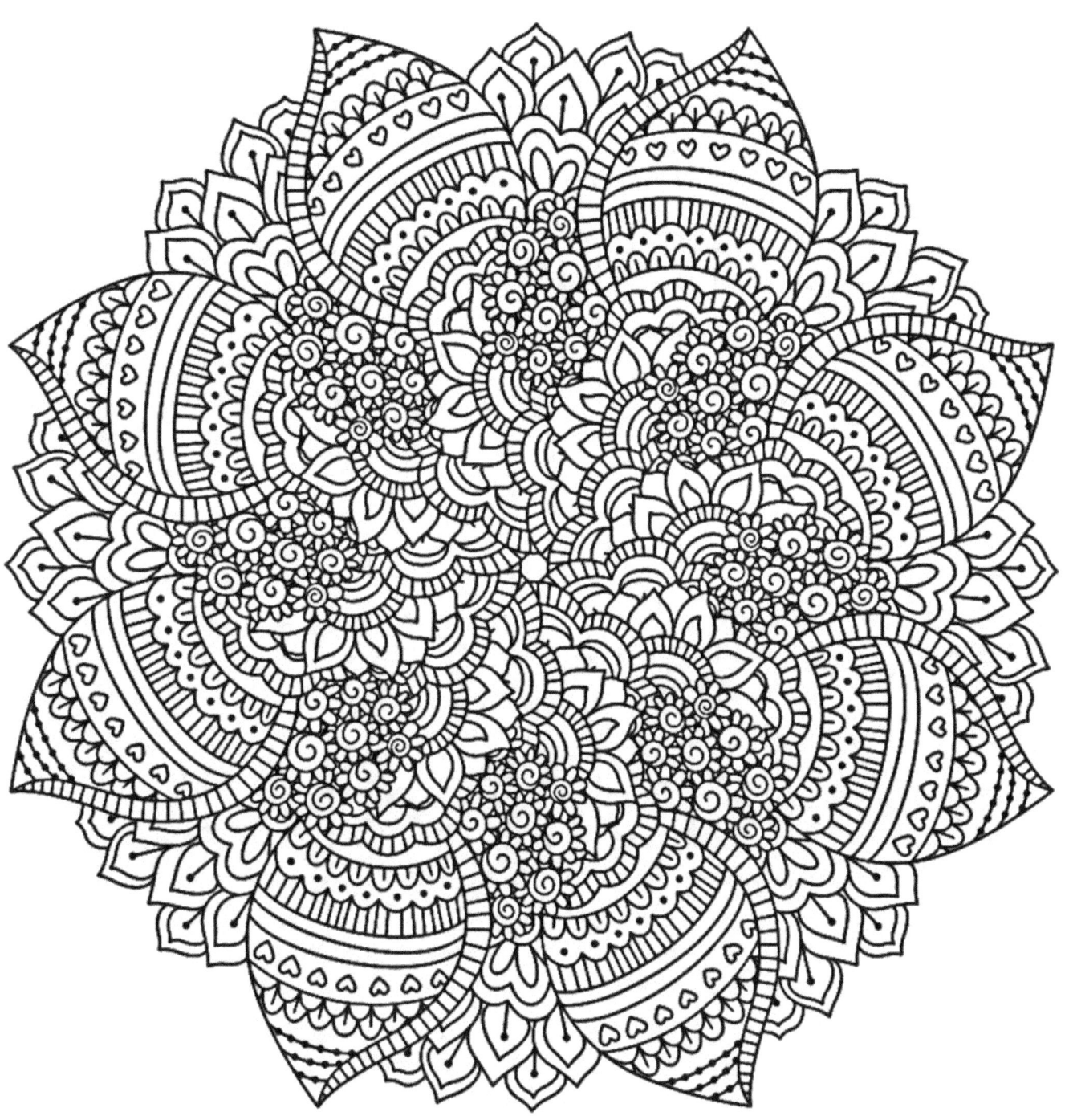

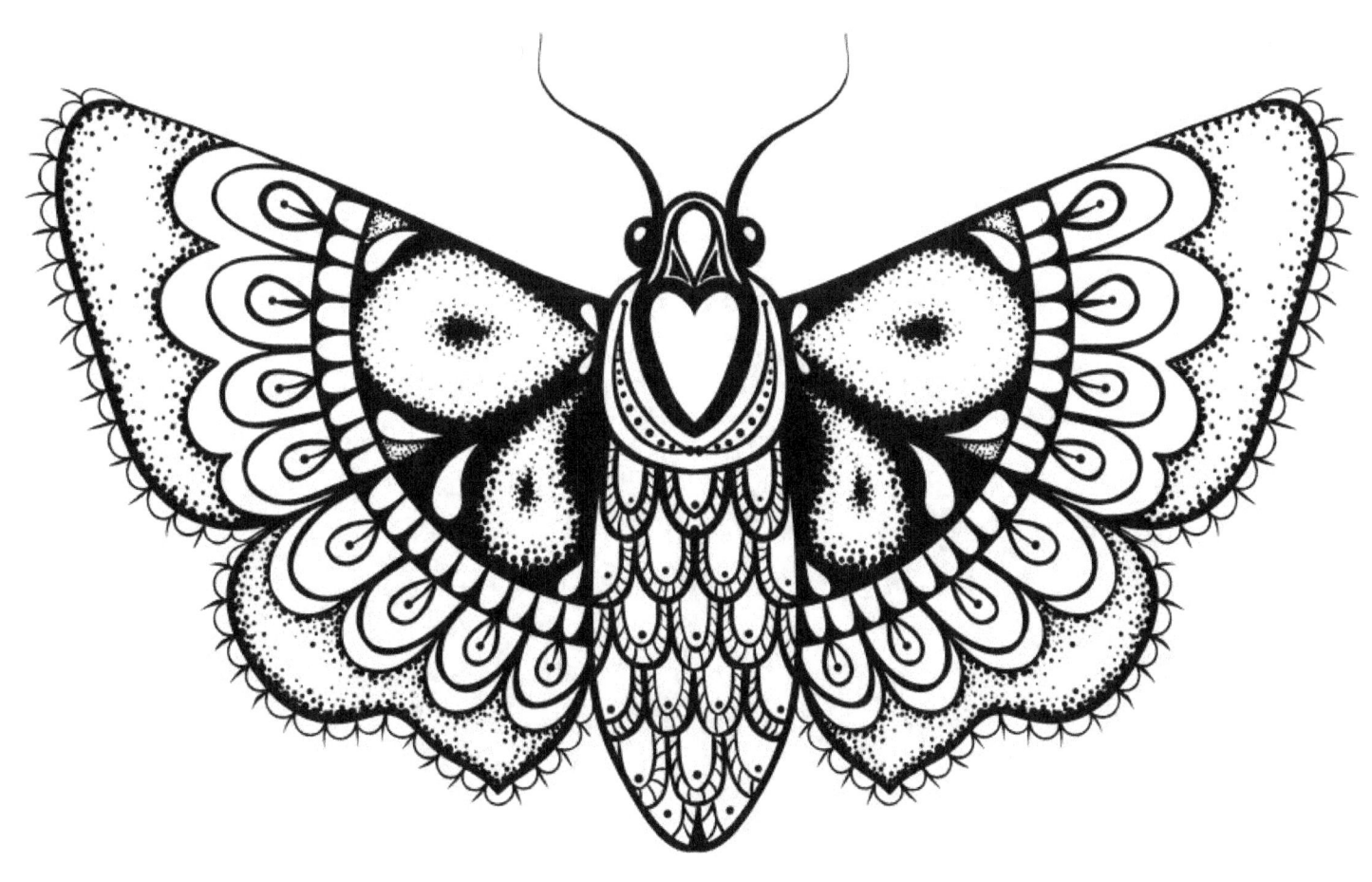

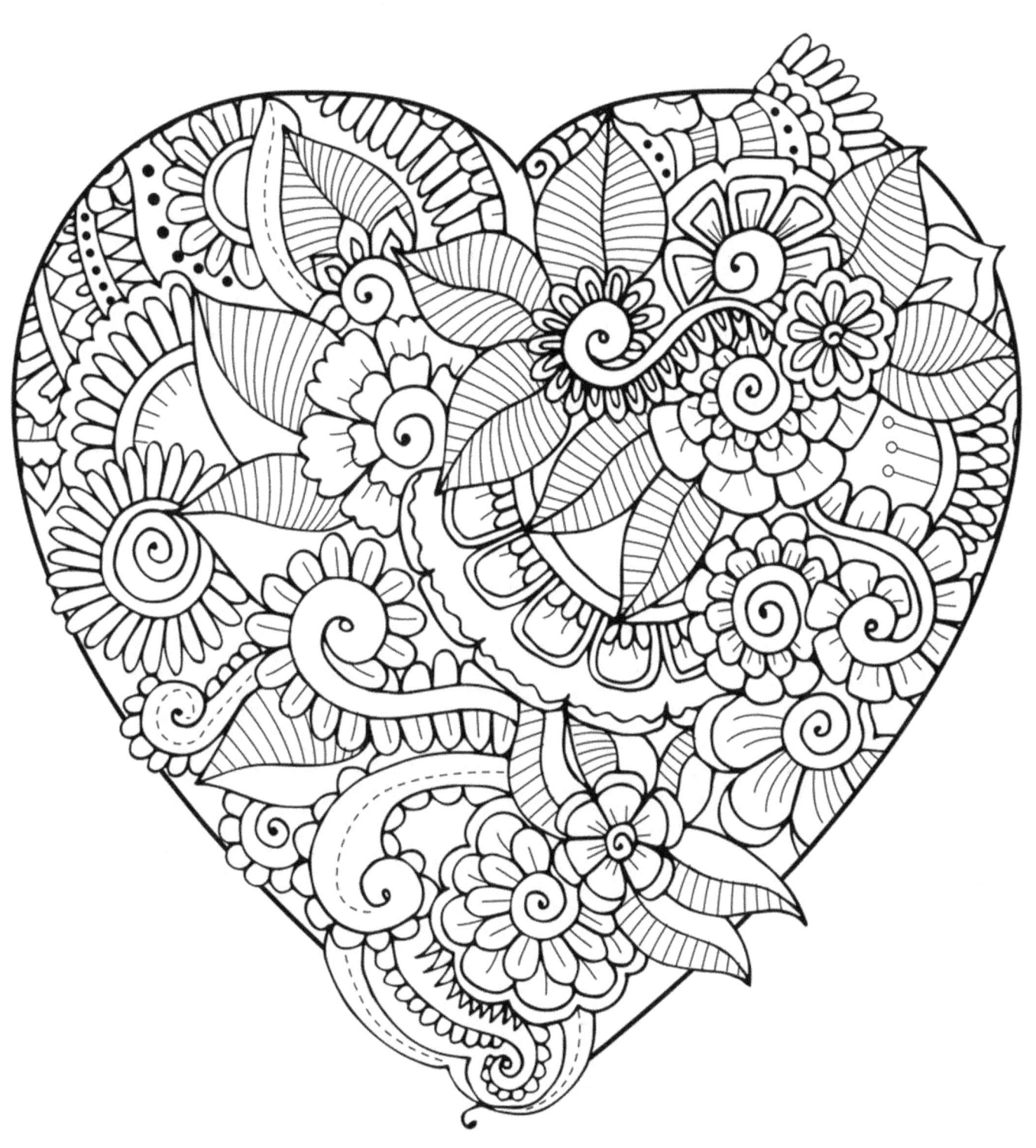

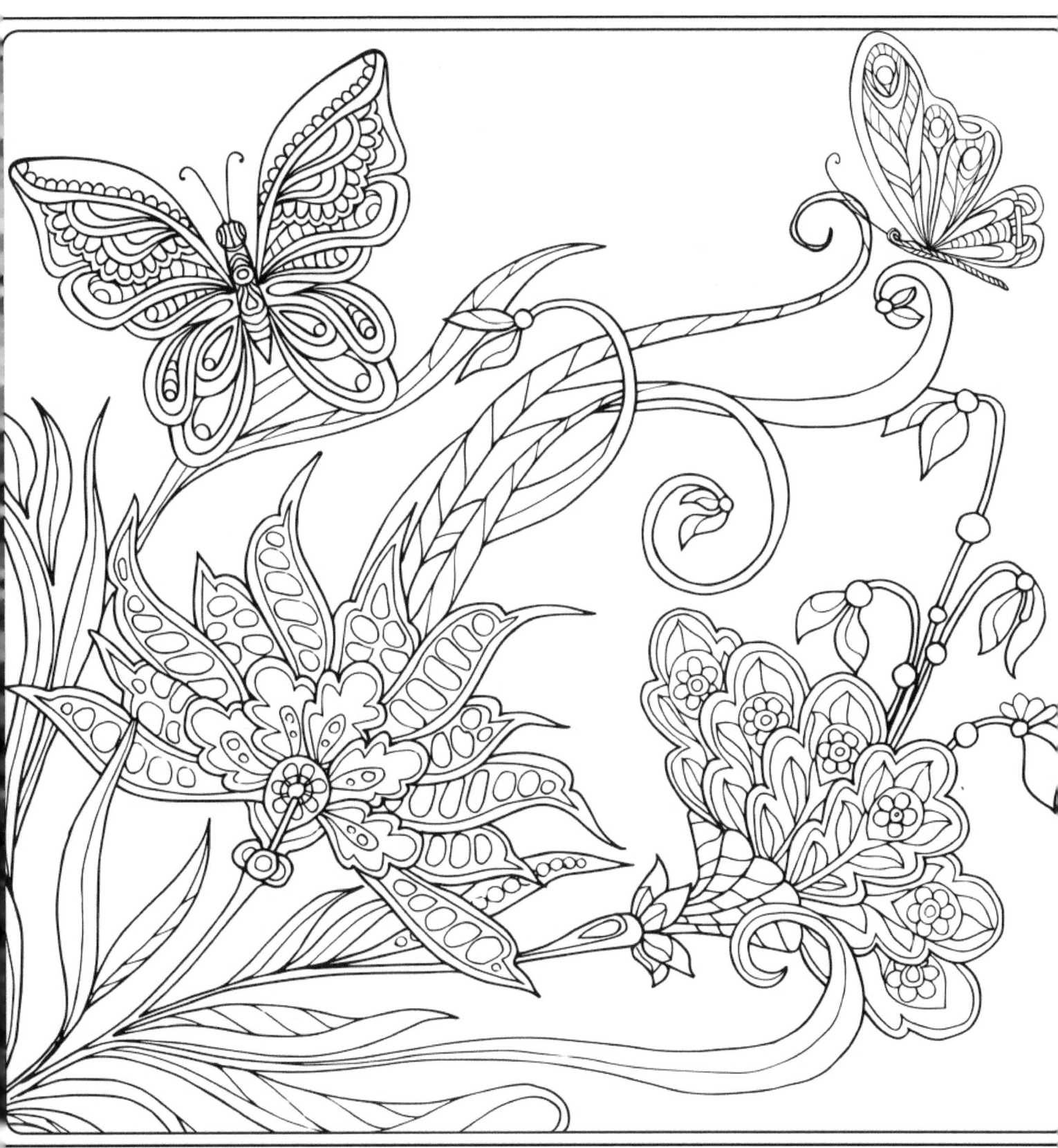

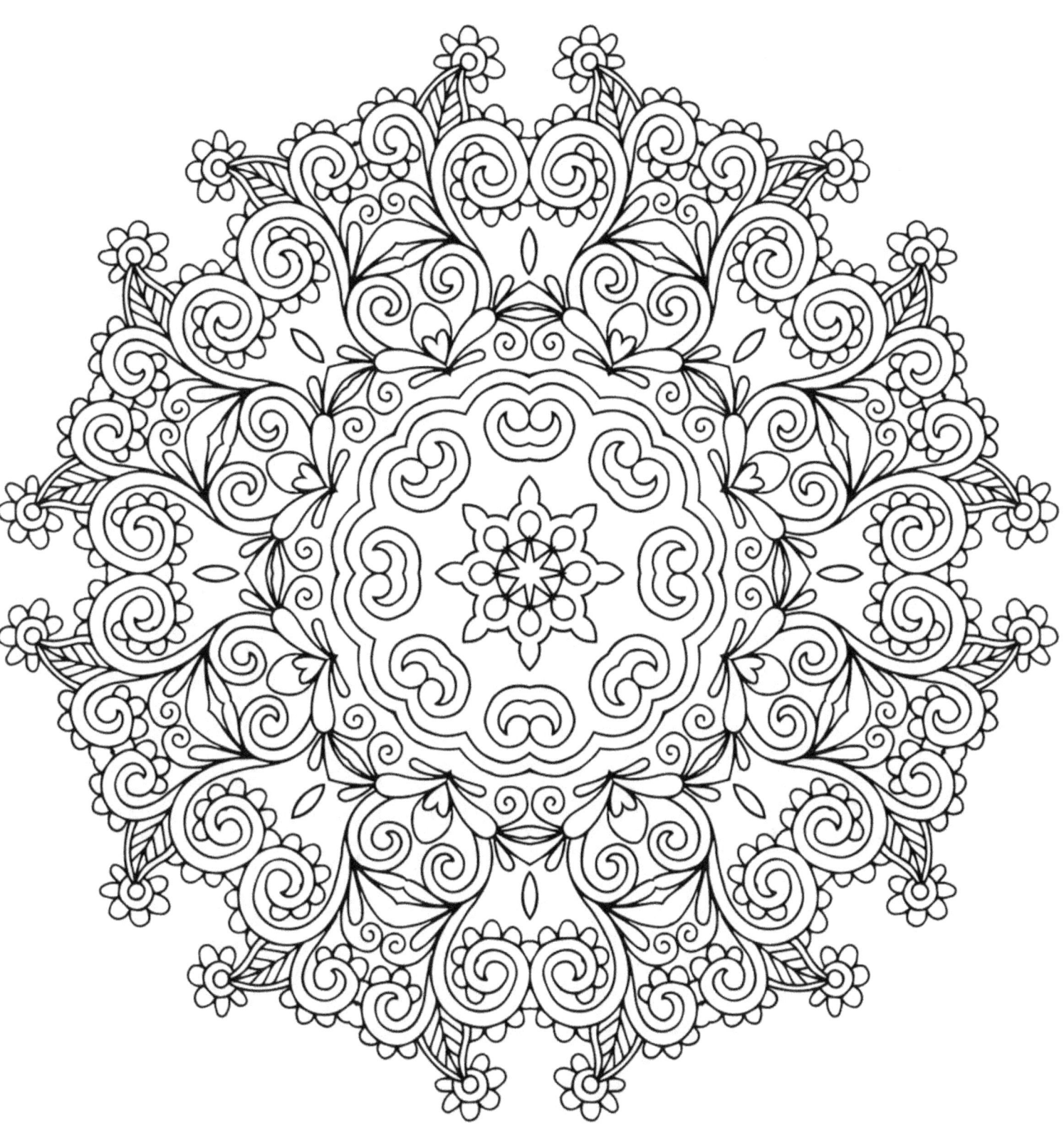

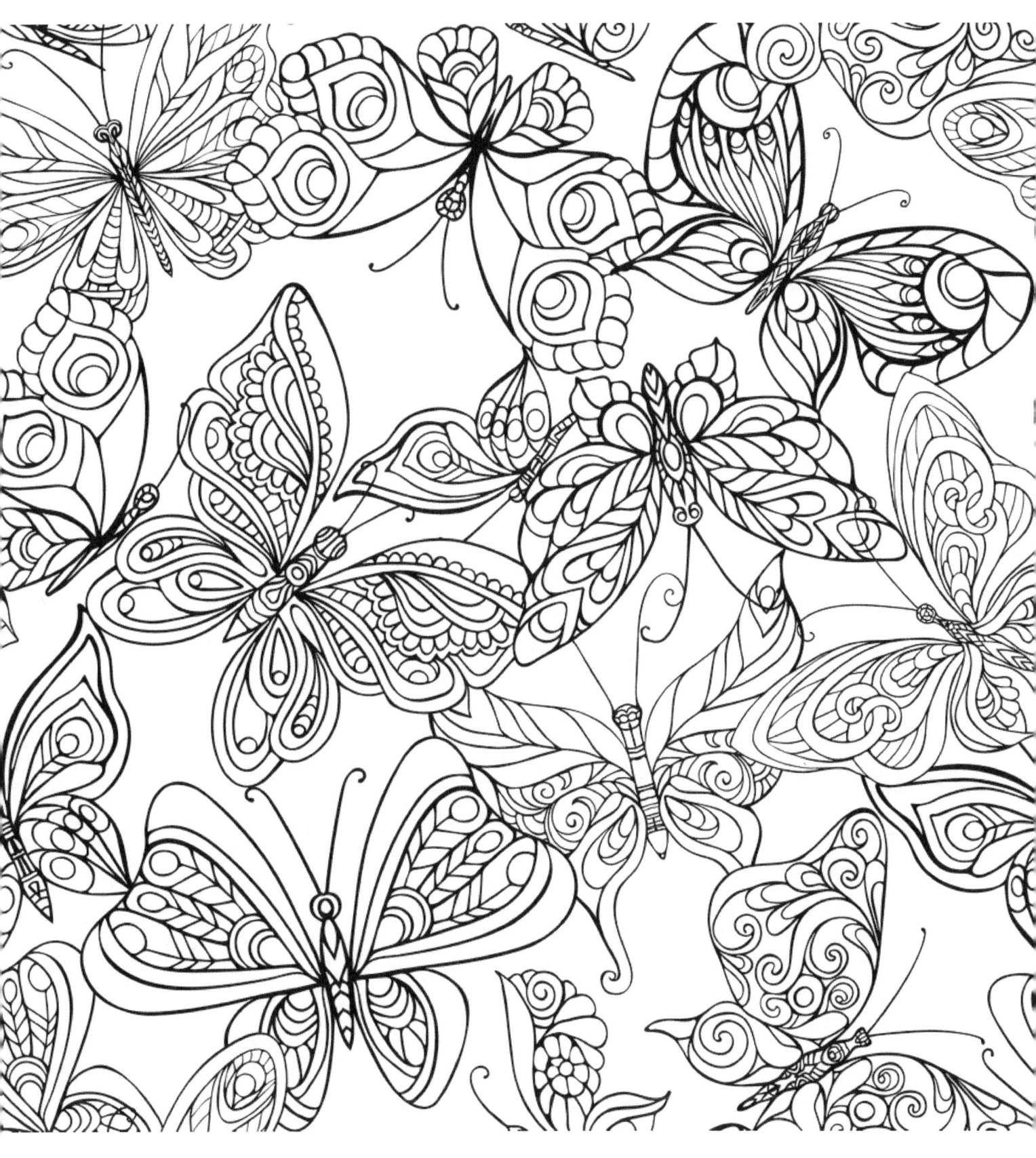

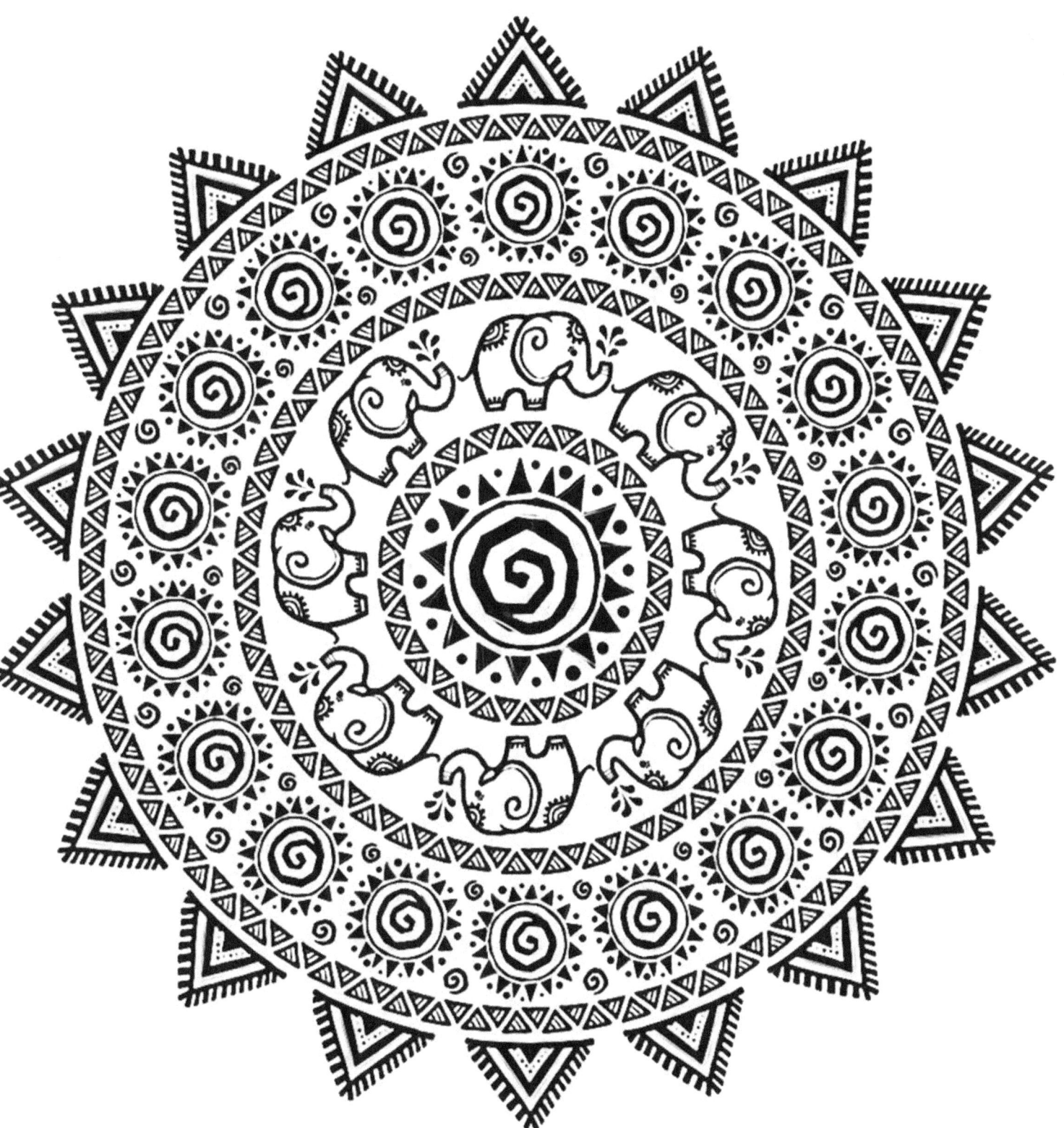

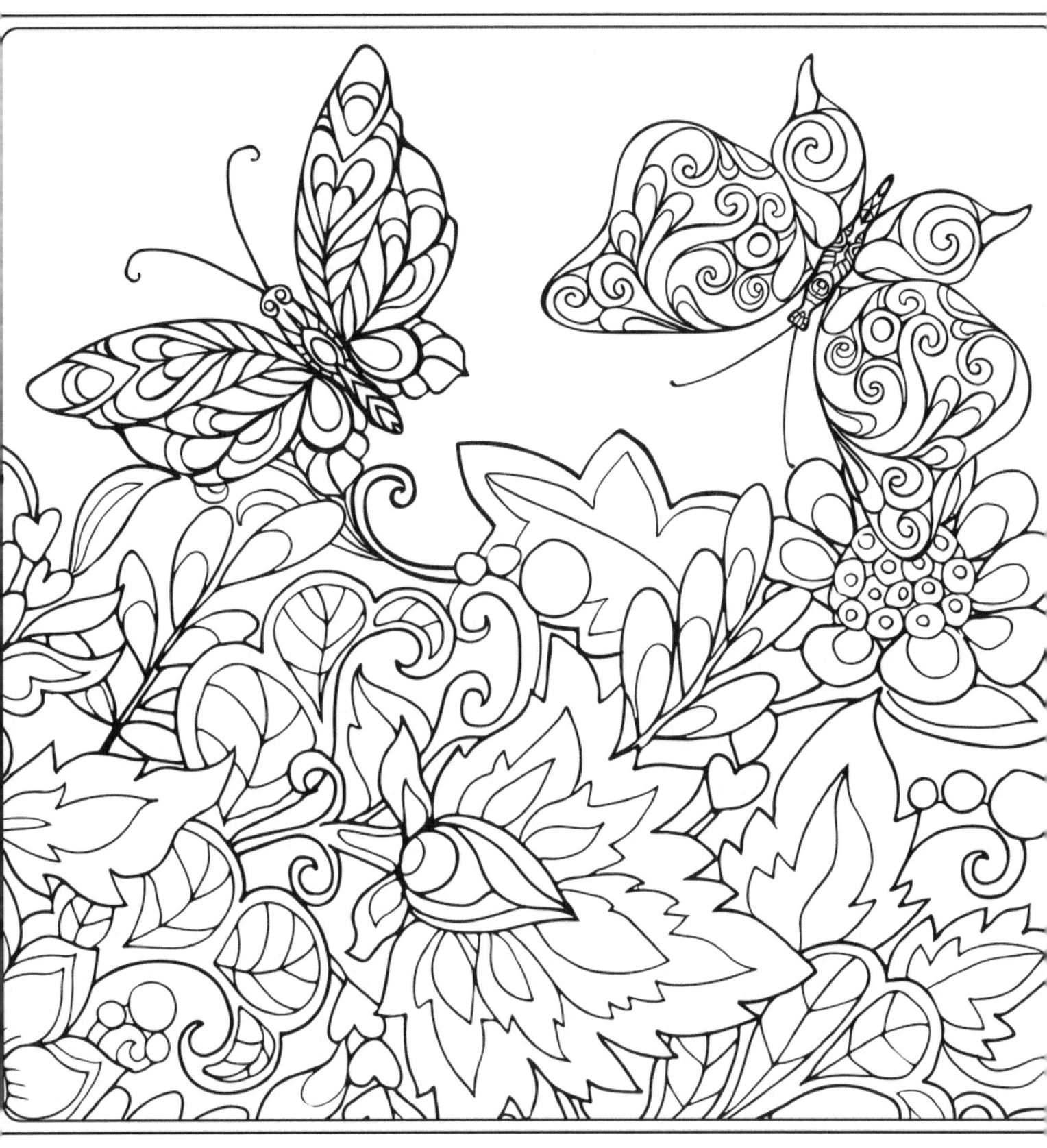

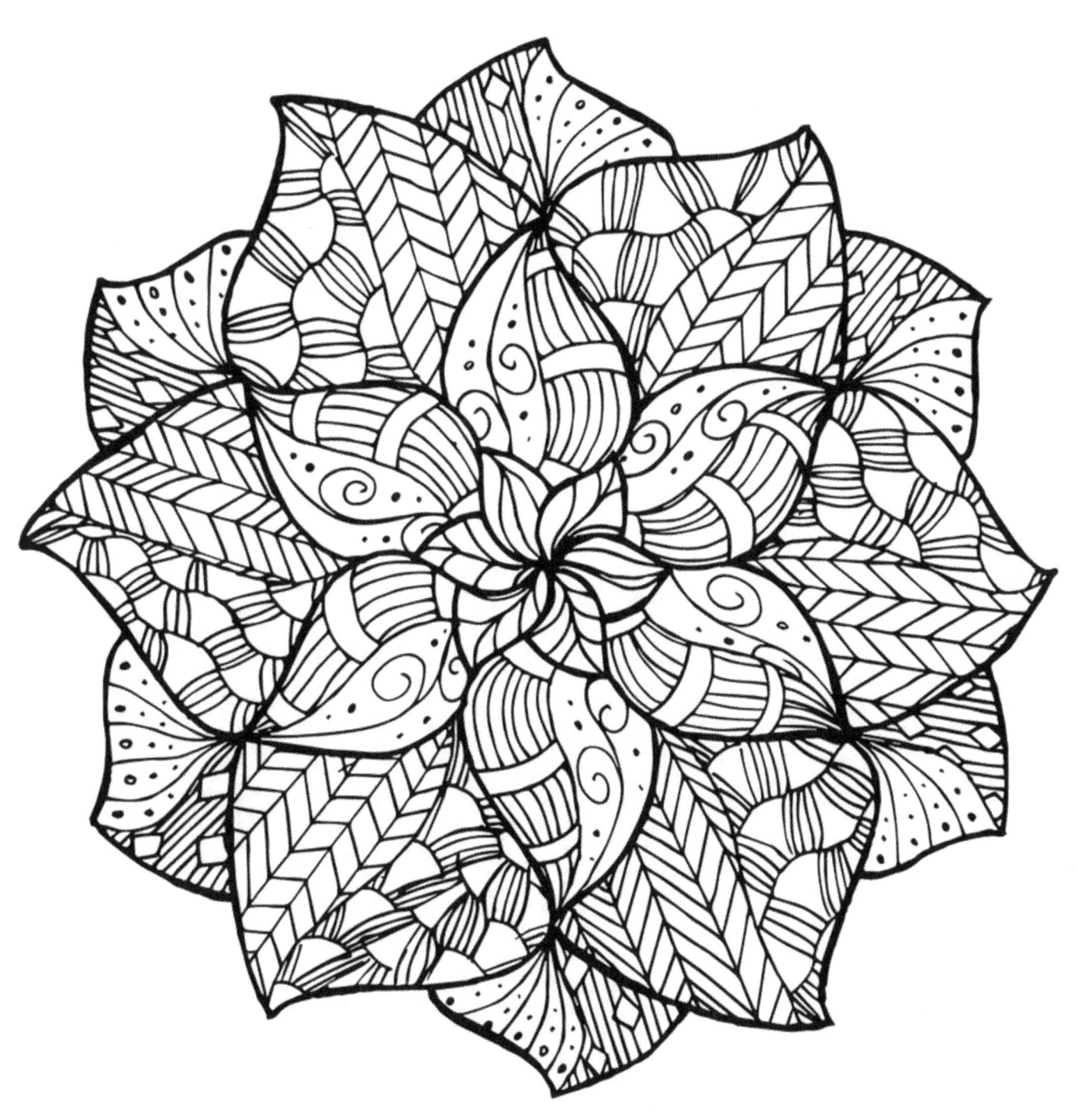

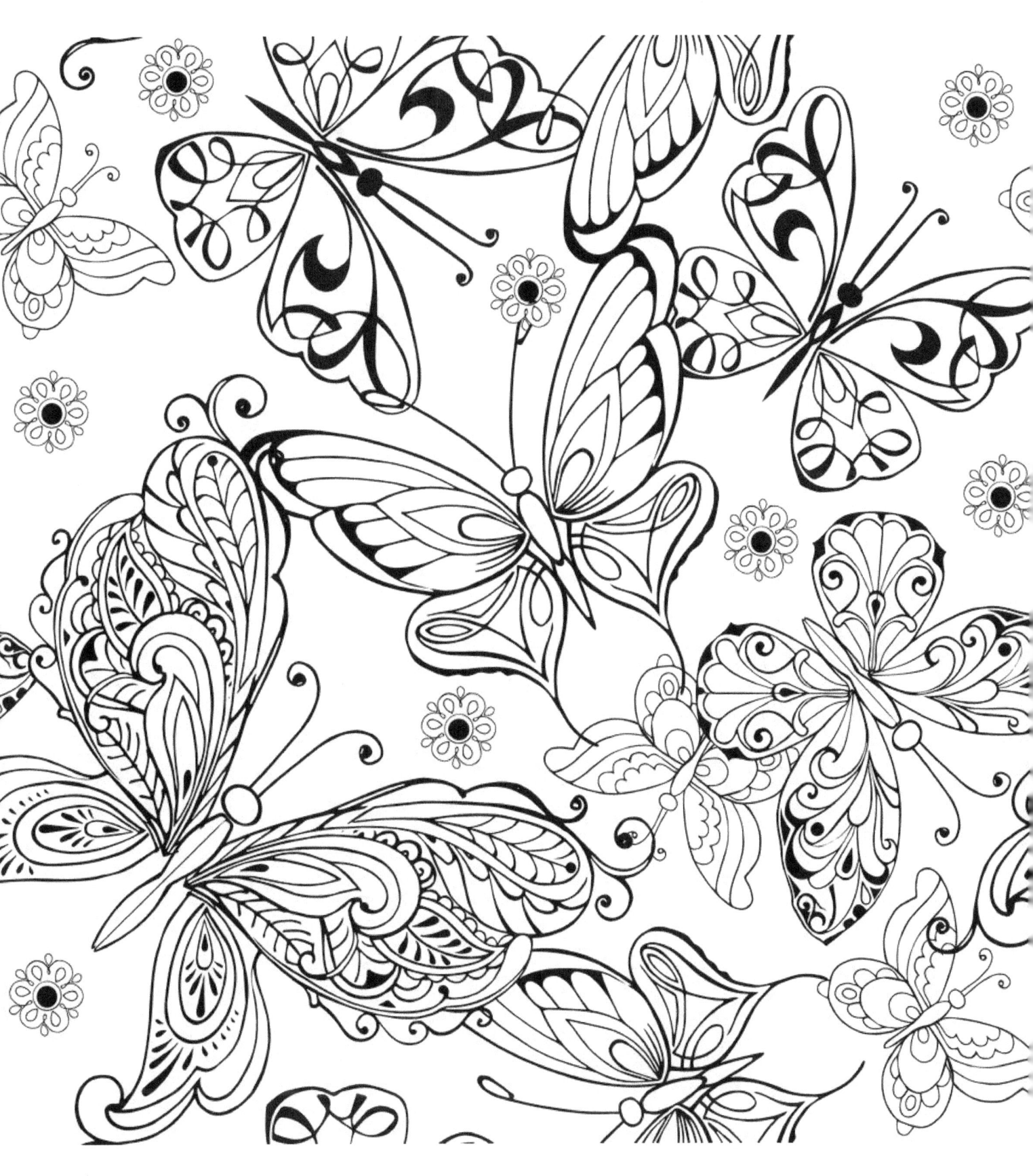

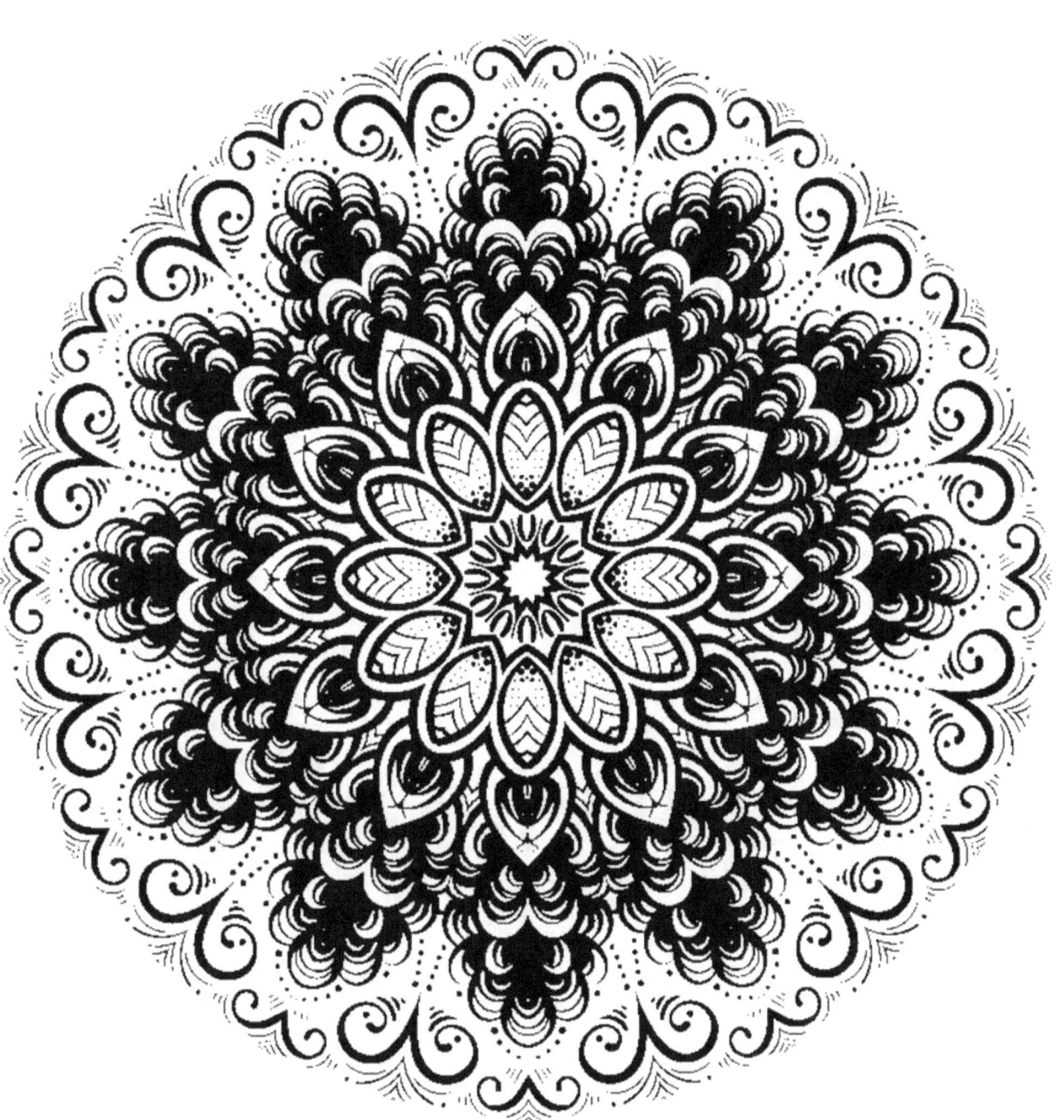

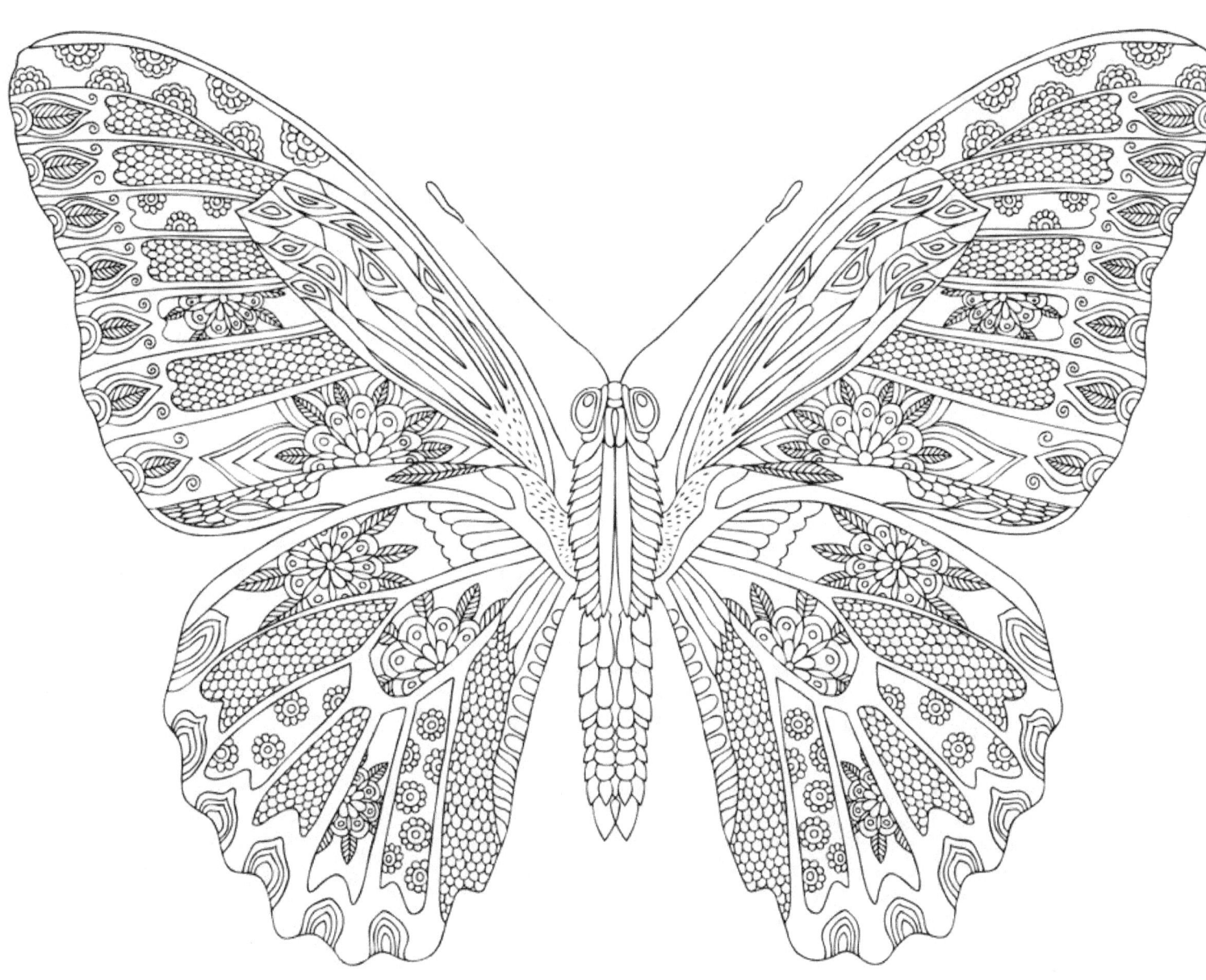

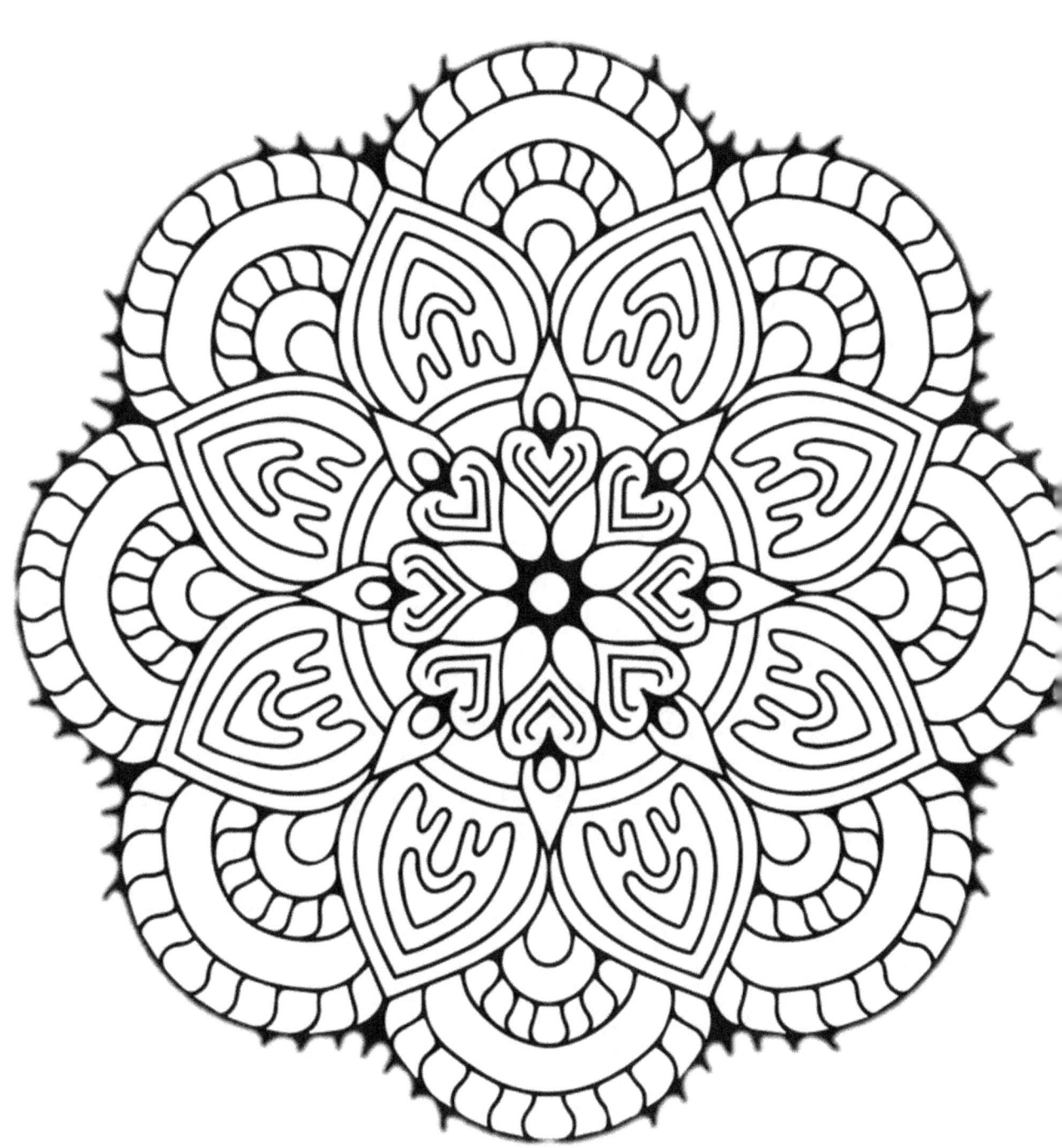

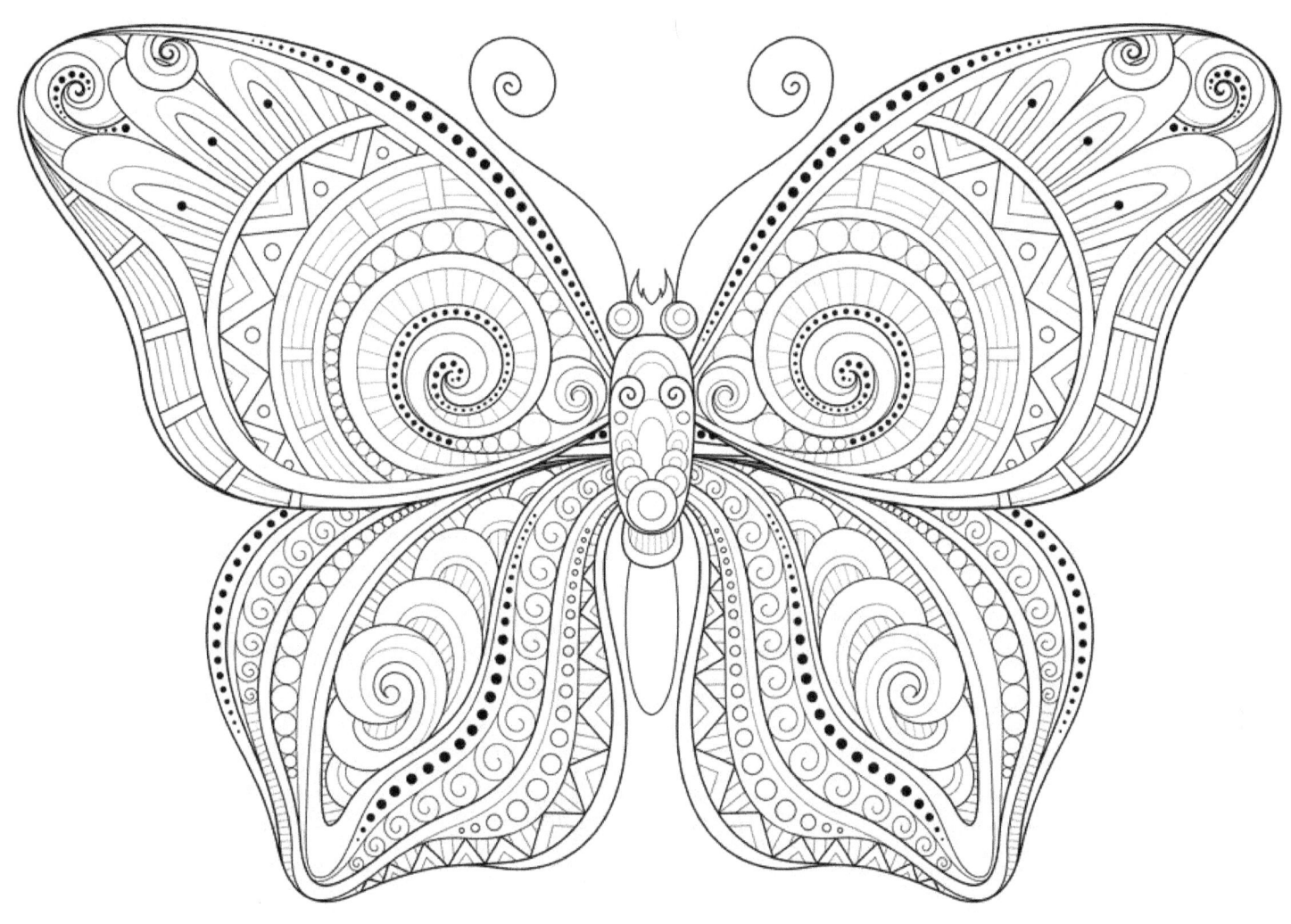

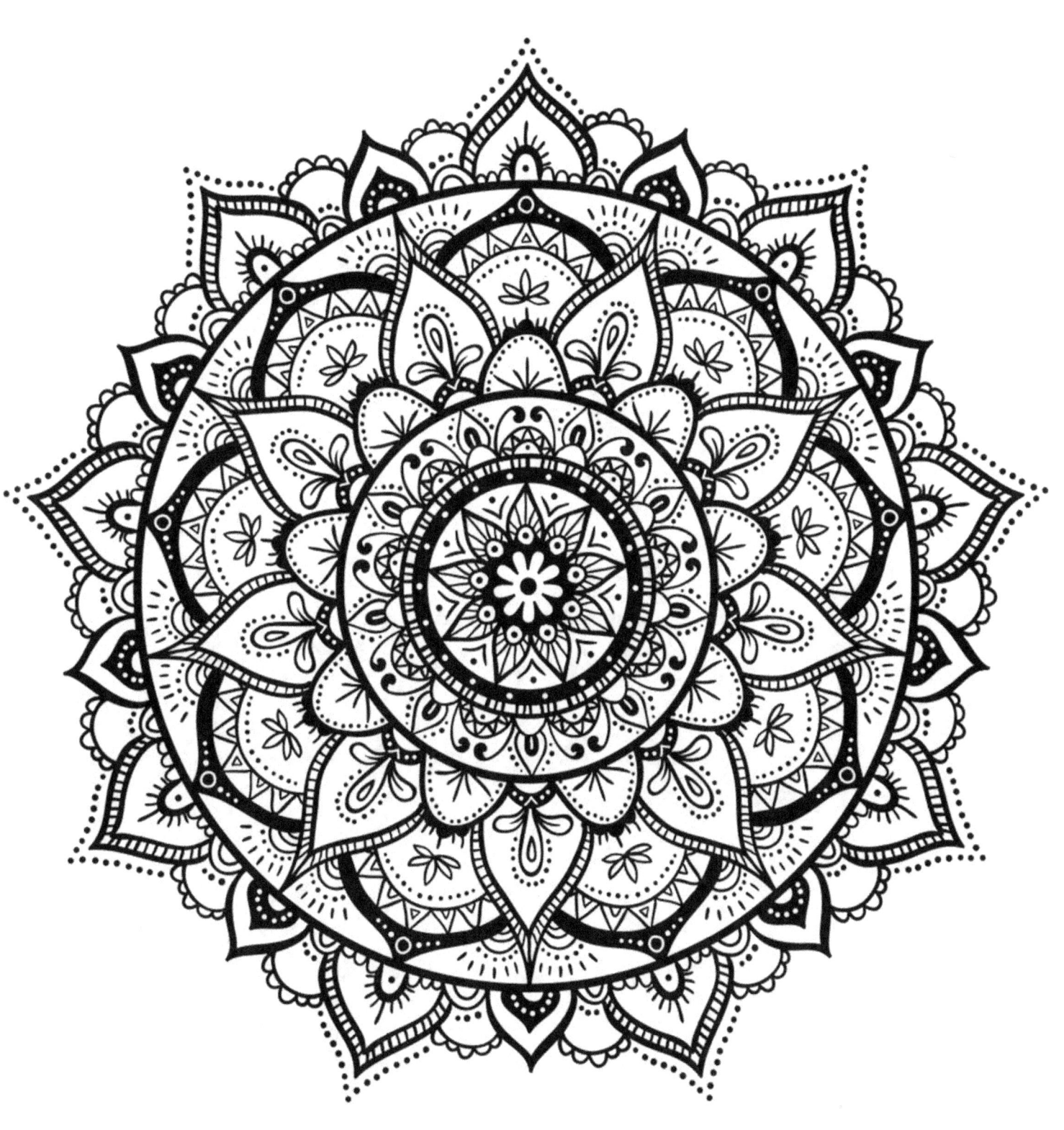

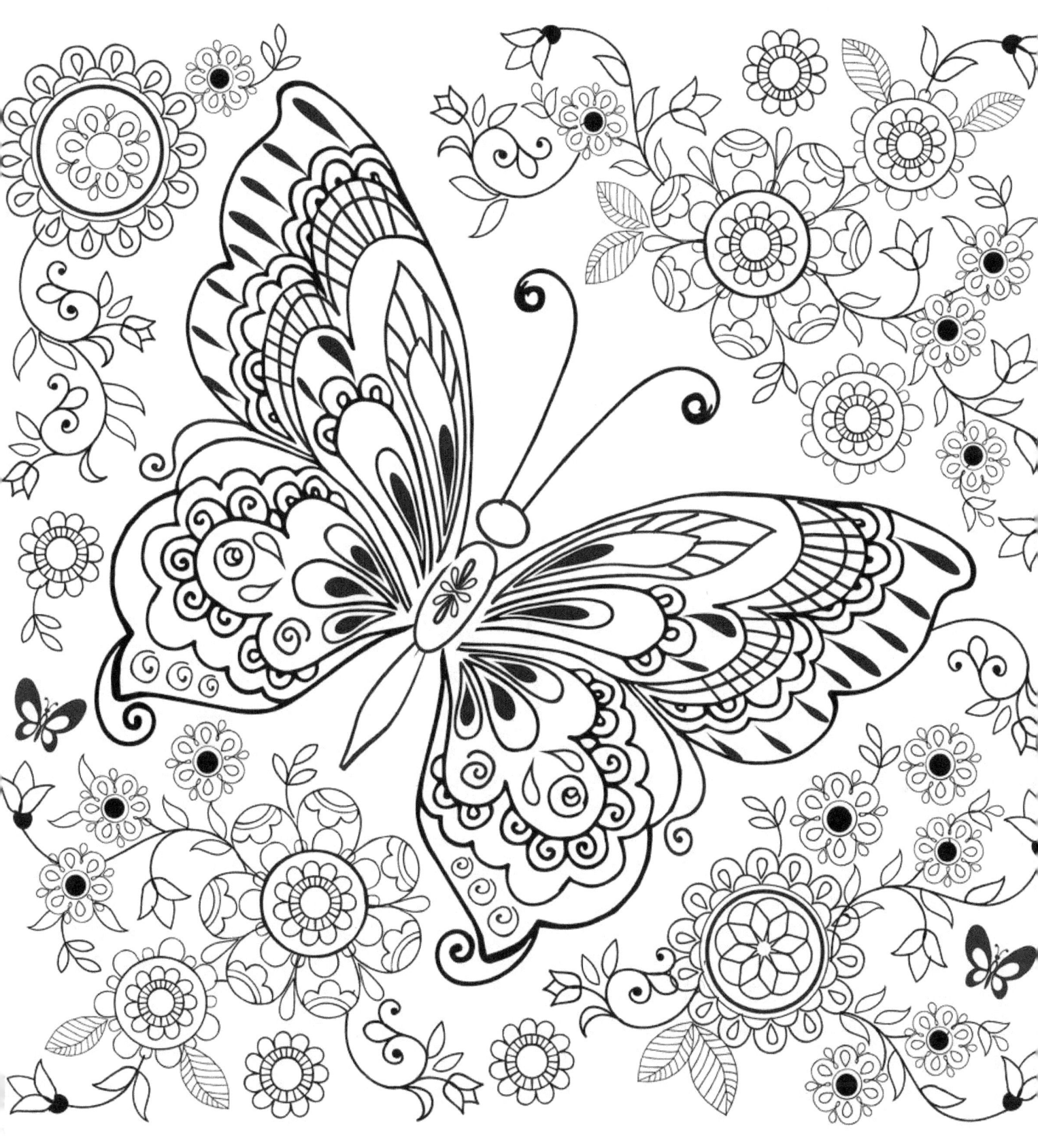

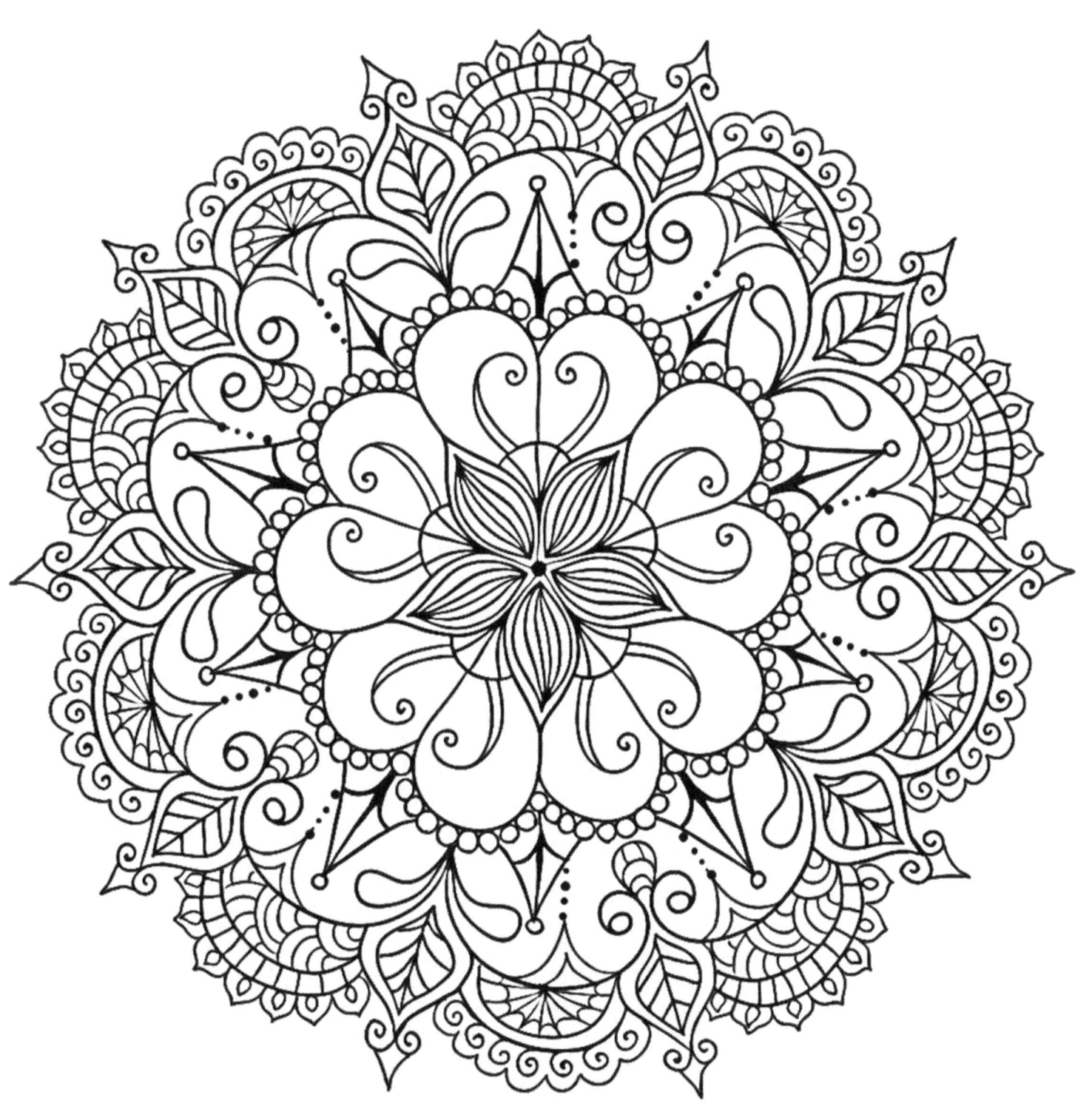

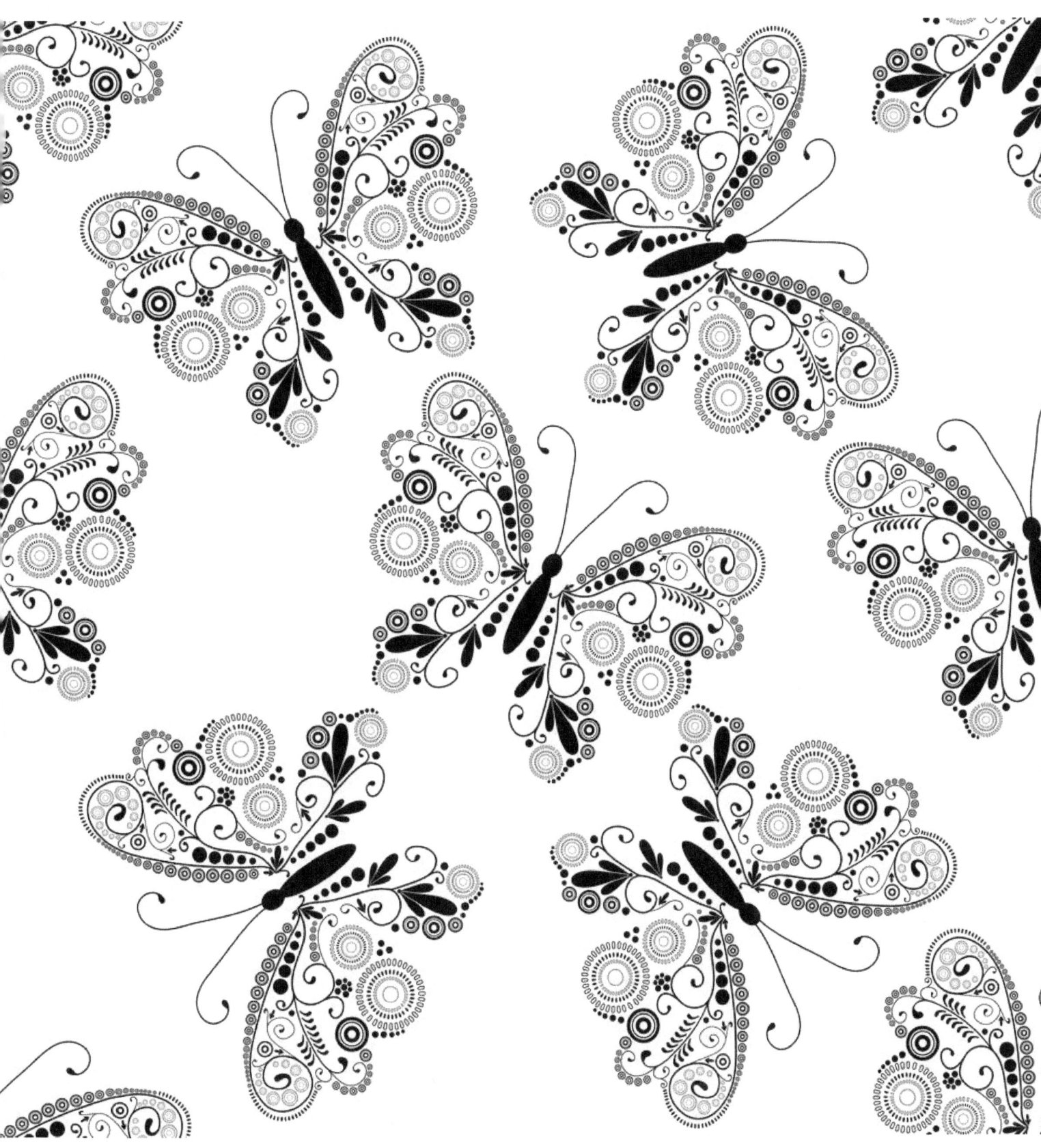